AF597953

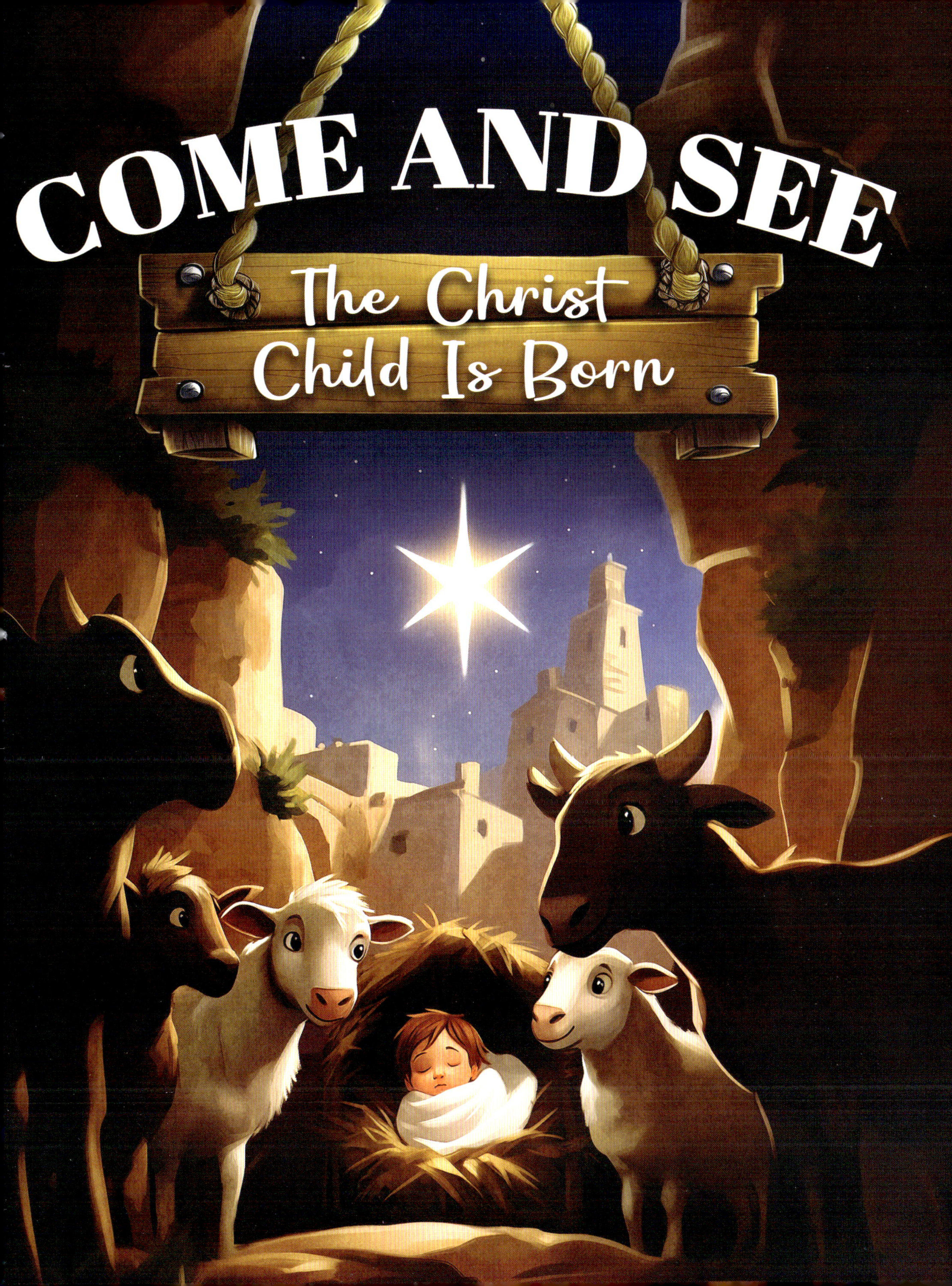
COME AND SEE
The Christ Child Is Born

Dedicated to my grandchildren, whose smiles light up the world. And also dedicated to my Lord and Savior, whom I choose to follow now and always.

—Michelle

Dedicated to my amazing kids, who are already on their path to greatness. You amaze me everyday!

—Shawnda

© 2024 Michelle Porcelli
Illustrations © 2024 Cedar Fort, Inc.
All rights reserved.

No part of this book may be reproduced in any form whatsoever, whether by graphic, visual, electronic, film, microfilm, tape recording, or any other means, without prior written permission of the publisher, except in the case of brief passages embodied in critical reviews and articles.

The opinions and views expressed herein belong solely to the author and do not necessarily represent the opinions or views of Cedar Fort, Inc. Permission for the use of sources, graphics, and photos is also solely the responsibility of the author.

ISBN 13: 978-1-4621-4800-4
ebook ISBN 13: 978-1-4621-4840-0
Published by CFI, an imprint of Cedar Fort, Inc.
2373 W. 700 S., Suite 100, Springville, UT 84663
Distributed by Cedar Fort, Inc., www.cedarfort.com

Library of Congress Control Number: 2024944656

Cover design and interior layout and design by Shawnda T. Craig
Cover design © 2024 Cedar Fort, Inc.

Printed in China

10 9 8 7 6 5 4 3 2 1

Printed on acid-free paper

COME AND SEE

The Christ Child Is Born

written by Michelle Porcelli art by Shawnda Craig

CFI · An imprint of Cedar Fort, Inc. · Springville, Utah

Welcome to Bethlehem

Come!
See the busy people
run about the town,
greeting friends and guests who
have come from all around.

Come and see lovely Mary

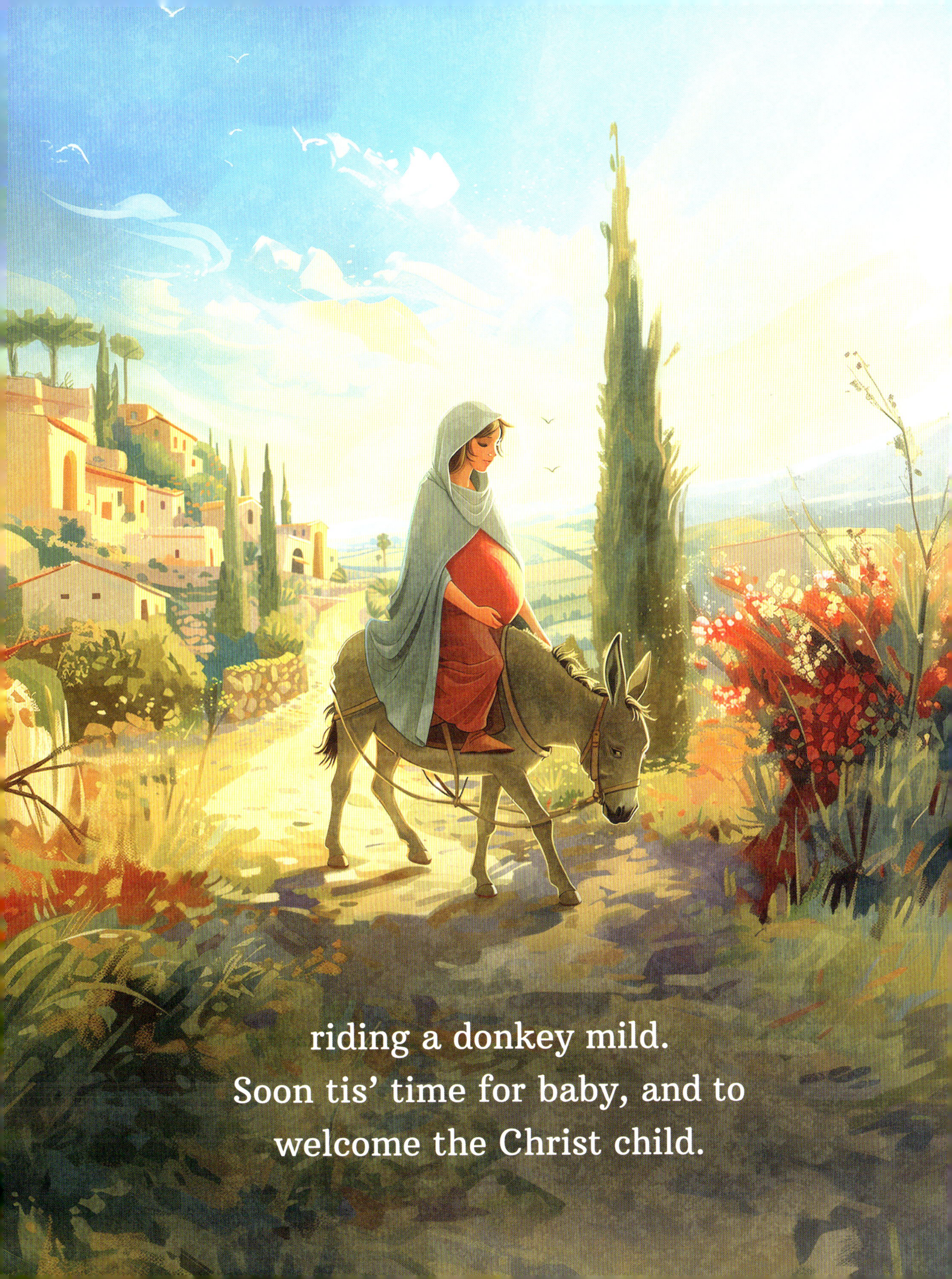

riding a donkey mild.
Soon tis' time for baby, and to
welcome the Christ child.

Come and see the innkeeper

who makes up all the beds,
turns away the young couple,
no place to rest their heads.

Come and see the shepherds

when an angel beckons them, bearing truth. The Savior will be born in Bethlehem.

Come and see kind Joseph

helping Mary rest her head.
Baby Jesus soon sleeps here,
a manger for his bed.

Come and see the cattle and
the little sheep just shorn.

For they know the time is
nigh for Jesus to be born.

Come and see the wisemen,

watching stars this special night.
They notice a new light shining,
one star much more bright!

Come and see the Shepherds
running down the the hill with glee.
For an angel had beckoned to them,
"COME AND SEE!"

Come and see the Christ child
is born! Shout it out with glee.

He is here to save us all, to
lead, and set men free.

Come and see the baby

who now lays atop the hay.
All will honor His birthday. We
call this Christmas day!

Come and see Christ learn and
grow in wisdom and in truth.
Wisemen bring small gifts to
share, to help while in his youth.

Come and see sweet Mary
who is proud of her wise son.
She guards Jesus dearly
knowing He's the chosen one.

Come and see! He teaches
all to walk the narrow path,
so we too can work and
receive 'all the Father hath'.

Come and read His life story,
for all can choose to hear.
He is the way, the truth, the
light. He is always near.

Come and see the children
now turning to Jesus' light,
showing honor for Christmas
that sacred, holy night.

Come and see Jesus showing love to us each day. He is the Savior of the World. He will light the way!

AF597952

Katrina Daschner

BURN & GLOOM! GLOW & MOON!

Sternberg Press
kunsthalle wien

Edited by
Övül Ö. Durmuşoğlu

Works Presented

Preface

We are very grateful that Kunsthalle Wien has had the privilege to host "BURN & GLOOM! GLOW & MOON! Thousand Years of Troubled Genders," the most comprehensive exhibition of artist Katrina Daschner's work to date. The show was carefully put together by guest curator Övül Ö. Durmuşoğlu, who brought her extensive expertise and open method to the project. It encompassed works from the 1990s to the present, tracing a line of intersectional queer interest that continues to undermine (neo-)liberal, heteropatriarchal conceptions of sexuality, gender, subjectivity, and relationships.

Daschner works with various closely interrelated media, ranging from sculpture, textile, music, performance, community-based work, and, most prominently, film, which sat at the heart of her show. As did collaboration, an integral and long-standing focus of Daschner's practice and a central interest of the program we seek to develop at Kunsthalle Wien.

In order to arrive at collectivity and collaboration, Daschner challenges the narrow space that normed, patriarchal subjectivities offer. Take, for example, her early works, like the collages (1999–2002) exhibited at Kunsthalle Wien, in which Daschner began experimenting with self-portraiture. The images, for which she posed with masks and different costumes, were taken with an analog camera, then cut up into fragments and assembled into hybrid bodies. For her, these collages represent early experiments with a "subject in flux." It doubles, triples, merges, and takes on different attitudes and gendered roles. In the end, her self-portraits do not produce a single coherent subject, but rather split it open and let it bloom. The staging of differently gendered roles confronts their supposed fixity, as well as issues of desire, violence, and power. In doing so, these works are part of a legacy of various queer-feminist intellectuals and artists.

In 2001, Daschner, together with Johanna Kirsch and Stefanie Seibold, founded the performance space Salon Lady Chutney in a former hairdressing salon. The Salon, which was always meant to be temporary, offered a space for performance at a time when discussions around topics such as performance or gender hadn't yet reached the Viennese academies, and when there were practically no institutions or spaces dedicated to performance art in the city. Unfolding on two levels, with a large window front facing the street, the Salon comprised a stage, an exhibition space, and a bar. It could be adapted for all kinds of activities and learning—which, in addition to performing and displaying art, included intellectual exchange in the form of lectures or film screenings, and, of course, excessive partying.

Engaging with Katrina Daschner's work allows us a glimpse into where and how Viennese queer study—in the sense of learning together and producing knowledge outside of traditional academic avenues—took and takes place. Her show fell in line with an ongoing questioning at Kunsthalle Wien: What are the different legacies of queer-feminist communities and histories that remain hidden and unarchived, locally and beyond? How can intersecting generations of feminists be brought into dialogue, both to collaborate and to challenge each other? And what alternative pedagogies and ways of social world-building do particular artistic practices offer?

Upon entering Kunsthalle Wien's entrance area, where Katrina Daschner's exhibition began, visitors were greeted by a large wallpaper print showing a row of performers dressed in shiny red and black. They are holding each other close, heads buried in each other's wigs and shoulders. Only fragments of limbs and costume are visible, there are no faces or other features that would make a person identifiable. For Daschner, this mass of bodies (a choir from her film *Flaming Flamingos,* 2011) resembles a collective being, a collective head that thinks and feels together.

In her practice, this collective body comes together rather than already being together. Here, desire is not exclusively given in the human but acts more like a pulse that permeated the exhibition space and put its elements into relation. Props, costumes, animals, synthetic material, performers, the cinematic image, color, refracted light—they all interact. Daschner makes use of desire's movement, a push and pull of attraction and repulsion. It was the haptics of her imagery, her search for something like a tactile gaze, that largely animated the space.

"BURN & GLOOM! GLOW & MOON!" allowed us, at Kunsthalle Wien, to yet again engage in a specifically local, community-based practice that expands toward an experimental way of life, encompassing many earthly things, moving beyond just the human. Katrina Daschner lets us dream and swerve, but her work also reminds us of the time and care that actual community-building necessitates, as well as of ambivalences, violence, and power, which all need to be worked through in relationships. We hope to learn from that and want to thank and cherish the work that went into putting together the exhibition at Kunsthalle Wien as well as this catalog.

–What, How & for Whom / WHW
Artistic Directors
Kunsthalle Wien

–Andrea Popelka
Assistant Curator
Kunsthalle Wien

Environ-
ment

of
Senses

Dreams That Can Be Camp and Damp …

Introduction by

Övül Ö. Durmuşoğlu

And then the day came,
when the risk
to remain tight
in a bud
was more painful
than the risk
it took
to Blossom.

Anaïs Nin, "Risk"

"Some nights you are the lighthouse / some nights the sea / what this means is that I don't know / desire other than the need / to be shattered & rebuilt," writes poet and novelist Ocean Vuong in his poetry collection *Night Sky with Exit Wounds*. If there is a basic definition of desire in the queer sense, notwithstanding all of its differences in shades and colors, it is indeed the space to be shattered, rebuilt, and reborn. In times of uncertainty loaded with so many changes yet to come—in the time of monsters between the dying old world and the arriving new world struggles—the powerful queer subjectivity of shattering and rebuilding is not limited to bodies, communities, and their genders. It is a fundamental way of understanding and practicing life energy in order to create more space for joy, resistance, and resilience.

Some encounters are magical from the very first moment, and so was ours with Katrina Daschner in 2018 during the opening of her exhibition for Diagonale Film Festival in Graz. The senses of glam, power, fragility, and sensuality alongside the continuous states of becoming and its subtle violence embraced each other in textures that could not be separated in that small yet powerful setting. I wondered why I hadn't seen her work before. Then I realized it was because I was not an avid follower of Oberhausen Film Festival and other important experimental film gatherings. Experimental film gave Daschner a unique fluid space to dive into her imaginary and reenact its idiosyncratic forms, visions, and appearances within her LGBTQIA+ community in Vienna. The conversation that began that day became life-changing for both of us, as she and WHW collective invited me to accompany Daschner on a major journey weaving her largest monographic exhibition at Kunsthalle Wien. The home studio—familiar and so unknown at the same time—soon became a magical portal; we revealed unspoken threads among multiple layers of her practice as we spoke of living life queer and making queer lives mutate.

> "Thousand years of troubled genders / Now we're here to live it all / Past and future all together / Tears for the absent and beloved / Burning pearls like glooming stars / Glowing eggs of mooning spiders / As love will tear us all apart"

In 2007, Daschner sang these transformative lyrics to the melodramatic song "Tears for the Absent" with her band SV DAMENKRAFT (together with Gustav and Sissy Boyz). The song is from the album *Orlanding the Dominant: A Queer Burlesque,* which is based on Virginia Woolf's novel *Orlando* (1928) and inspired the title of the exhibition, "BURN & GLOOM! GLOW & MOON! Thousand Years of Troubled Genders." The tone of the queer theory agenda in arts and culture was already set and defined by Judith Butler's now iconic *Gender Trouble* (1990) and Eve Kosofsky Sedgwick's *Epistemology of the Closet* (1990), followed by Jack aka Judith Halberstam's *Female Masculinity* (1998) and José Esteban Muñoz's *Disidentifications: Queers of Color and the Performance of Politics* (1999). Now, almost two decades after Daschner and her band performed "Tears for the Absent," we are still here to live it all, past and future together, more than ever.

"BURN & GLOOM! GLOW & MOON! Thousand Years of Troubled Genders" is followed by this publication, which desires to continue the journey of the exhibition on paper. We joyfully created an immersive environment of senses, textures, and feelings, journeying through over two decades of intersectional and queering practices in film, performance, sculpture, community work, and music. The new text Amelia Groom penned for us on the glitter syntax, the extended dialogue between Daschner and her longtime collaborator Rike Frank, and the reprint of a precious text by the late Tim Stüttgen are accompanied by material research and in-depth studio dialogues on queer and lesbian feminist, anti-racist situatedness in life and work. In the setting that we created together with Monika Rovan, the monuments of white patriarchal heteronormativity were dismantled stone-by-stone with pain and joy.

Throughout the summer of 2022, this glitter and glam environment hosted thousands of local and international visitors and gave them a not-so-easy-to-forget exhibition viewing experience; even for those who were already familiar with Daschner's work, it was a brand-new understanding that collapsed the boundaries of stage, film set, studio, and white cube into one fluid performative space. The old work and the new work met with each other in this exclusive space and redefined each other's borders, strengths, and fragilities. By expanding the space with further historical material and different footnotes, the publication becomes more than a regular exhibition catalogue.

Daschner scripts and enacts various proposals of corporeal fluidity herself and with the help of her queer friends and comrades. The stylized performances challenging patriarchal mores and their everyday norms in Western society enable her to play with the boundaries of human and non-human, natural and artificial. They expose the fictitiousness of the gendered binary, its institutions, and the prejudices it generates, freeing the body from patriarchal, heteronormative codes. Starting in 1997, she began to sew and crochet her *Zuhälter*, colorful toys made out of a variety of materials, to wear on her body for various collages and performances. The *Zuhälter* enable actions of shattering and rebuilding queer desire in Daschner's artistic universe. They hold together new identities in transition. Like her masks, they signal the constant yet transforming presence of the Other, the foreign constitutive part of the self-image, which is indispensable for Daschner to discuss queerness.

In her performances and video works, the stage becomes the setting for a precarious desire for (in)visibility and, at the same time, an endless yearning for rebirth. The performers mostly perform in silence for a potential audience in empty seats. They demand that the inbuilt patriarchal normative codes of potential audiences change. The late Tim Stüttgen touches on the core of Daschner's artistic strategy in writing about her film trilogy *NOUVELLE BURLESQUE BRUTAL* (2011): "Deconstructions and reconstructions of otherwise sexist genres are used for new self-conceptions and self-assured empowerment, not just to criticize normative or even violent images and acts—such as those supplied by mainstream porn and its many at times explicitly misogynous varieties—but also to counter them with self-selected affirmations." On photo paper and later textile, Daschner's stylized acts merge with her provocative and titillating image politics—she merges incomplete stories of love and pleasure, violence and resilience, death and rebirth into each other with her endless cutting and pasting.

Scheherazade's incomplete stories, one night after another, save the lives of young women in the classic *One Thousand and One Nights*. And Daschner is a generous storyteller who wants to intervene in linearity in a similar way. During one of our conversations, she shared that her turn to experimental filmmaking with *Hafenperlen* (Harbor Pearls, 2008) was inevitable because it gave her the opportunity to unite and create space for all the motifs, forms, and various genres she researched in her collage and textile work into one cosmos. The spatial grammar of installation didn't have the freedom she created for herself with the enactments possible in experimental film. Furthermore, her idiosyncratic engagement with film shows how installation-oriented and filmic practices can merge and transform each other in alternative visual, temporal, spatial, and corporeal forms. As she has mostly continued to work with the same team and protagonists, she consequently has strengthened the ties between queer kinship and storytelling through collective labor and imagination. The publication makes the figures of the protagonists more visible.

Daschner's artistic acts function like threads attaching her stories, stages, and characters together. They highlight queer desire as a force of life and remind us that we can all be the lighthouse or the sea or the jellyfish. Threading, circling, and wandering were the strategies through which the exhibition "BURN & GLOOM! GLOW & MOON! Thousand Years of Troubled Genders" moved, enacting new connections among Daschner's works. In response to her dreamy settings, certain powerful components of films and performances became evocative installations themselves and touched each other in a new way. Symbolic scenes from her films *Hiding in the Lights* (2013) and *Powder Placenta* (2015) adorned the walls, a sitting area responded to *Plum Circus* (2019), the choir from *Flaming Flamingos*, the third part of the film trilogy *NOUVELLE BURLESQUE BRUTAL* (2011), greeted visitors at the entrance of the exhibition, and the flittering shiny confetti and applause from the film *Hiding in the Lights* took over the foyer. Those who followed the thread entered the main exhibition hall from a big *Vagina Dentata* (2022), similar to the one from which Daschner and her protagonists jumped in *Pferdebusen* (Horse Boobs, 2017). In addition, new textile collages and sculptures wrapped themselves around a core of filmic work, including *TANZ2000* (DANCE2000, 2000) and her latest film *Golden Shadow* (2022), which spoke with her early collage work.

Daschner confronts, mediates, touches, embraces, and dreams. Some of her dreams are very camp, and some quite damp. She is like the unique four-headed sphinx in the Ancient Greece and Egypt collection of Kunsthistorisches Museum. She has more than one head, one voice, and more than one riddle to trouble those who want to seize power. In order to do that, she also sculpts a collective genderqueer body—a queer performance squad that changes in size for different performances; sometimes six, sometimes thirty womxn accompany her in various moments. The collective performance space Salon Lady Chutney was opened on March 8, 2001, by Daschner in collaboration with Johanna Kirsch and Stefanie Seibold. It was made up of a stage, a bar, and an exhibition space. In 2009, with the motto "More is more and less is just less!", CLUB BURLESQUE BRUTAL, at brut Wien, introduced bizarre, glamorous, intelligent, and funny burlesque shows to Vienna with a wonderful troupe of queer performers —from Vienna's diverse queer scene— hosted by Daschner as Frau Professor la Rose.

"BURN & GLOOM! GLOW & MOON! Thousand Years of Troubled Genders" came at a critical time of public empowerment for womxn (cis and trans), LGBTQIA+, crip, and BIPOC communities in the contemporary art world. And it also reminded visitors that the "rainbow" had been and will continue to be much more than a marketing tool; this public empowerment happened because of many invisible faces and voices who fought for it with their lives in different parts of the world. This book is dedicated to them alongside the various communities that were part of the process of its making. We hope that it will provide an insightful guide to Daschner's unique cosmos for curious audiences, artists, scholars, and researchers.

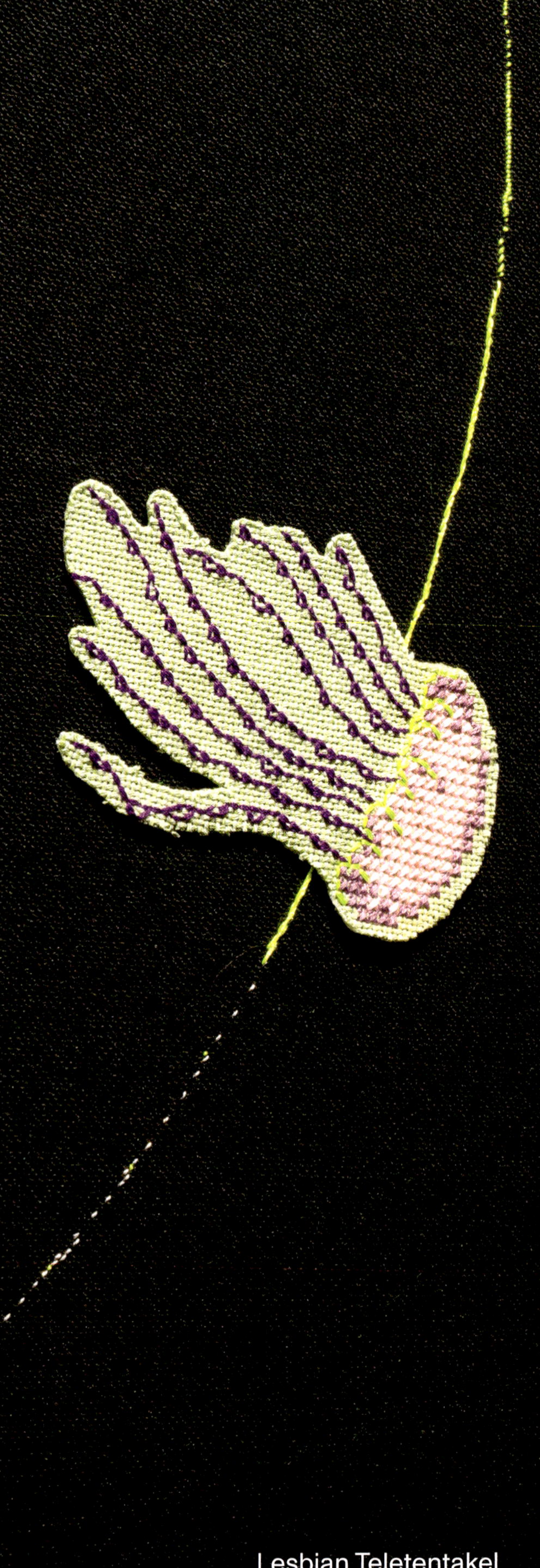

Lesbian Teletentakel

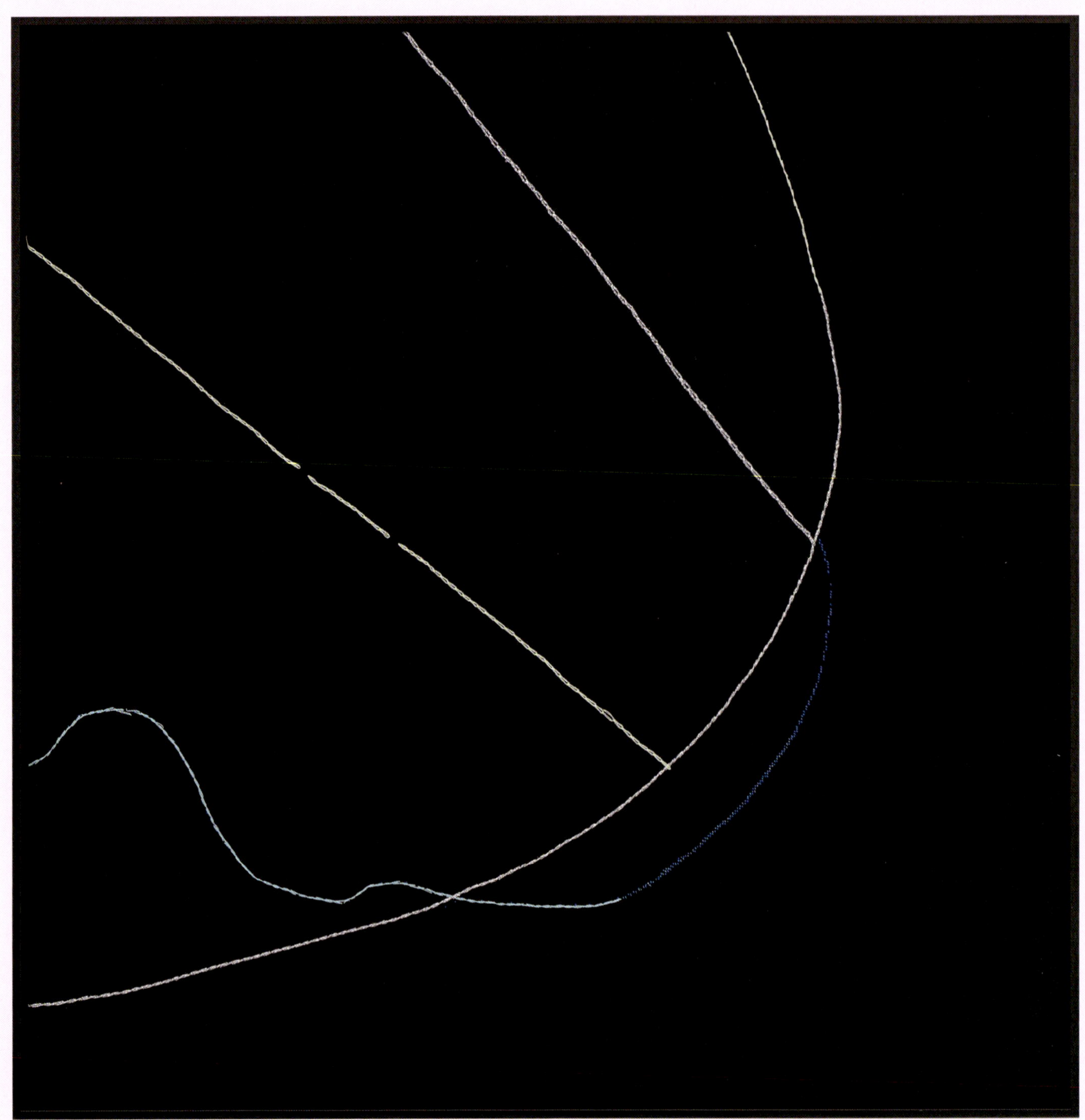

1
1

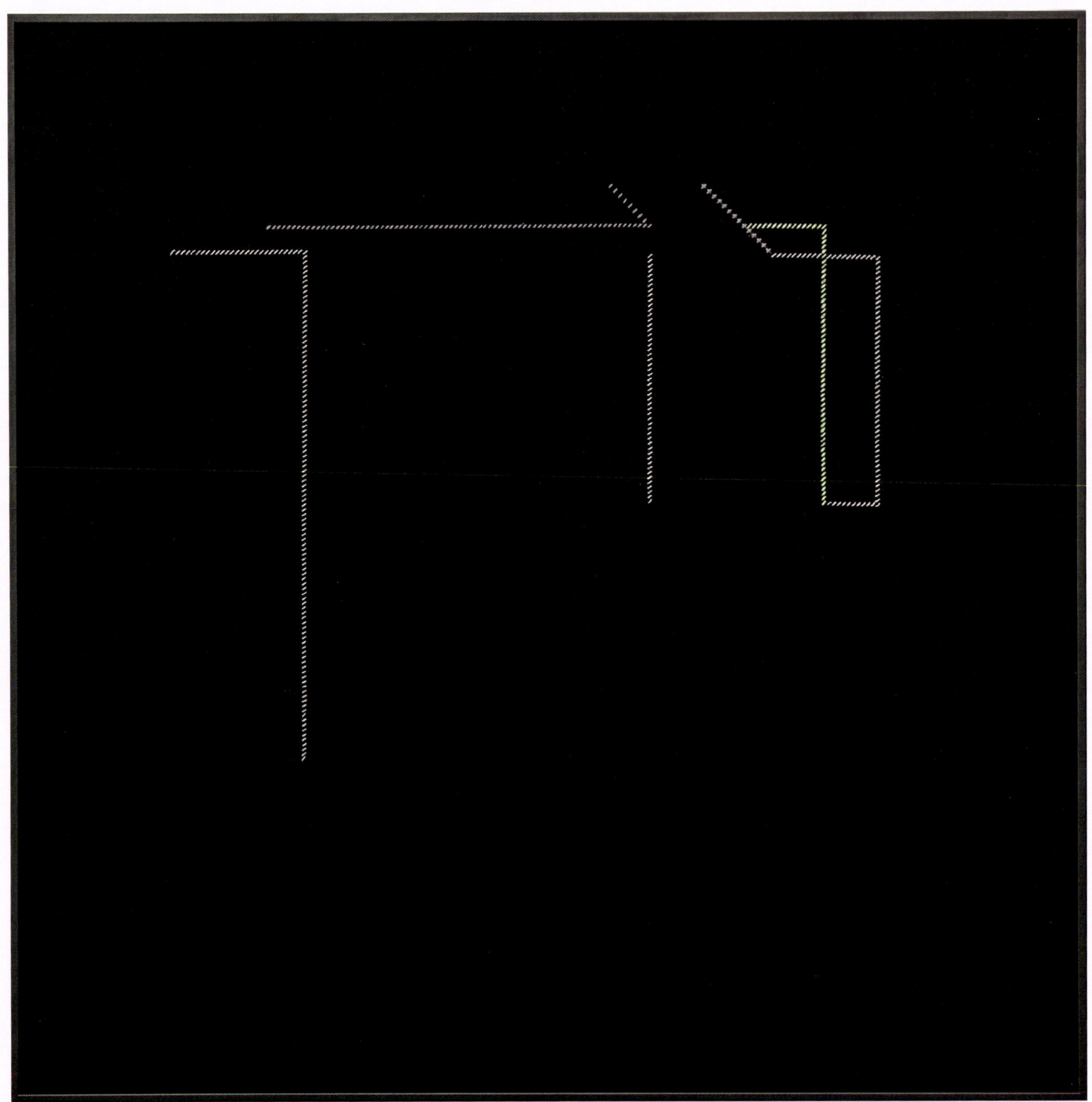

Performances

Femmelesque. Co-ordinates of a Dyke-Tease Idiom

Text by

Tim Stüttgen

The following text is a shortened and slightly edited reprint of Tim Stüttgen's essay, first published in Katrina Daschner, *NOUVELLE BURLESQUE BRUTAL: A Trilogy by Katrina Daschner*, Salzburg: FOTOHOF edition, 2012.

Tim Stüttgen wrote about Katrina Daschner's *NOUVELLE BURLESQUE BRUTAL* (2011), a film trilogy in which the artist and the queer choir perform different variations of queer-feminist burlesque. Even though the films themselves were not part of the exhibition at Kunsthalle Wien, Tim Stüttgen's thoughts and contextualization of these works hit the center of the body politics at play in Daschner's overall practice as well as the works presented in "BURN & GLOOM! GLOW & MOON! Thousand Years of Troubled Genders."

The curtain rises. What do we see? What sort of saucy event have we been invited to? But perhaps we ought to talk of events, plural, and of invitations, plural, since we are witnessing a three-act show, a true trilogy that began with *Hafenperlen* (Harbor Pearls) in 2008 to culminate, three years later, with *Flaming Flamingos* (2011). The (supposedly) "low" culture being performed here is commonly referred to as striptease. The artist Katrina Daschner is not just showing us another sexual pose of the kind that art history has always morally lambasted—even if it did sell very well.[1] So this is not another variation on the "sex sells" theme, but something much more specific, something which in its most emancipated variation is referred to as Queerlesque.[2]

But one thing at a time. Who exactly is the invitation from? Is it the artist who in her works is just as capable of depicting the specific lustre of alternative sexual desire as she is of talking about patriarchal violence and abuse? Or is it the stage-savvy entertainer who has learnt to belly dance and likes to perform it at queer parties such as *Homoriental* (2001)? But perhaps we're also talking of the collective-backing string-puller who organized performative evening series at Salon Lady Chutney or the CLUB BURLESQUE BRUTAL to inject international variety into her home town's queer community? Well, Katrina Daschner combines the sums of all these individual parts [...].

It is important to note right at the outset that she boasts a certain autonomy vis-à-vis the traditionally sexist processes of striptease which, in sex work's patriarchal organizational structure, are sold for the benefit of men. And she also boasts a certain autonomy vis-à-vis the notorious and still powerful male gaze that structures the setting for sex work in the same way as cinema does, which has been analyzed by the feminist film theorist Laura Mulvey.[3] For in that context the woman puts on the feminine masquerade to act as the prosthesis and fetish of hetero-masculine lust and control.

By contrast Daschner constructs for herself her very own, out-and-out female-queer audience. But before we devote ourselves to the sway of her hips, we observers are faced with a female audience present in all her works that is reminiscent of the traditions of the Greek chorus—not without good reason. The history of theater tells us that these choruses appear at the beginning and the end of every play to comment on the dramatic action of the principal character. Where ritual dances for Greek goddesses once awaited the chorus's feedback, it is now the artist Katrina Daschner who is reliant on the comments of her queer-feminist entourage. Indeed, many of the notables who make up Vienna's diverse scene have gathered here. It signals a break with the look-and-lust structures that discipline the female body in commercial striptease shows. Daschner's audience could not be further removed from the normative trade-offs which organize the strip joints of the hetero sex industry. [...]

Let's remember that it was not for nothing that the lesbian philosopher Monique Wittig emphasized the fact in her works that lesbians were not in fact women.[4] And while that is not strictly true (the alliances between feminism and lesbianism are all too necessary today), it is a reminder that lesbian love undermines the reproductive relationship naturalized[5] by the heterosexual contract—with the woman doing the washing-up for the man, and producing the children, performing for him, and submissively submitting to him. In the affirmative (and protective) space created by the presence of other sisters, lesbian striptease cancels out the rules under which straight variants of sex shows operate. Where women otherwise get dollars stuffed into their G-strings to woo for attention in front of men and are made to enter into a competitive situation that is out of their control and based on rules still determined by the dominant male gender, Katrina Daschner creates quite a different backdrop in front of her queer chorus, entirely in keeping with the logic once stated by the theorist Teresa de Lauretis when referring to a "different scene"[6]—that of lesbian sexuality.

But when Daschner begins lasciviously to strip in these works, she is referring to several traditions of queer/feminist emancipation. First of all, there's the burlesque genre itself, which contrasts the straight schematics of the normative sex industry with different physiques (whether Black or white, fat or thin, young or old), different poses (such as ironic self-commentary or emancipated subtext), and different organizational forms (such as collective or performance troupes run by women)[7] . Then there is the tradition of pro-sex feminism and post-pornography, as expounded in particular by Annie Sprinkle and many others. Deconstructions and reconstructions of otherwise sexist genres are used for new self-conceptions and self-assured empowerment, not just to criticize normative or even violent images and acts—such as those supplied by mainstream porn and its many at times explicitly misogynous varieties—but also to counter them with self-selected affirmations. In her most prominent film *Annie Sprinkle's Herstory of Porn*[8] (1999) the American performance legend, who may rightly be referred to as the (grand-)mother of post-pornography, narrates her own career and opens up a pro-sex feminist space by overcoming the analogously blunt language of pornography to create a new grammar of marginalized practices and playful perversions. In so doing, she goes from supposed object to inventive subject, a process that has always been inconceivable in conservative anti-porn positions. Sprinkle herself once described post-porn as: "a new genre of explicit material that is perhaps more visually experimental, political, humorous, 'arty' and eclectic than the rest."[9] In 2011 this genre has given rise to a remarkable toolbox of queer practices, from dildo sex to cyber sex to post-gay S/M where prostheses, bodies, and technologies manage without the principle of the phallus and the number of sexual identities exceeds the notorious "two" many times over.

One of these many identities is that of the femme:[10] femme-ness occupies a specific position (long suppressed in the European context in particular) in the considerable quantity of subject conceptions that feel an affinity with the queer feminism movement. As the cultural commentator Margarita Tsomou once criticized in the queer magazine *Hugs & Kisses*: "We still owe a measure of recognition to the category of the 'femme'. Indeed we are long overdue in celebrating people who, despite the general hype surrounding drag-king culture and masculinization in

[1] A useful introduction to the contradictory logic of the art world of selling sex while making queer-feminist sexualities invisible can be found in Beatriz Preciado's text "The Architecture of Porn. Museum Walls, Urban Detritus and Stag Rooms for Porn-Prosthetic Eyes," in *Post / Porn / Politics*, ed. Tim Stüttgen (Berlin: b_books, 2010), 22–39.
[2] Introductory words on queer interpretations of the burlesque genre are to be found *inter alia* in: Malte Göbel, "Körpereinsatz," *Hugs and Kisses*, issue 2 (April 2004).
[3] Laura Mulvey, "Visual Pleasure and Narrative Cinema," in *Movies and Methods*, ed. Bill Nichols (Berkeley, CA: University of California Press, 1985).
[4] Monique Wittig, "One is Not Born a Woman," in *The Straight Mind and Other Essays* (Boston: Beacon Press, 2004), 9–21.
[5] See: Monique Wittig, "On the Social Contract," in *The Straight Mind and Other Essays* (Boston: Beacon Press, 2004), 33–46.
[6] Teresa De Lauretis, *Die andere Szene. Psychoanalyse und lesbische Sexualität* [The other Scene. Psychoanalysis and lesbian sexuality] (Frankfurt am Main: Suhrkamp, 1999).
[7] For a comprehensive introduction see: Jane Briggmann, *Burlesque—A Living History* (Duncan: Bearmanore Media, 2009).

[8] See Sprinkle's homepage, on which the film is still available: https://www.anniesprinklemovies.com/video/herstory/
[9] Annie Sprinkle, *Post-Porn Modernist. My 25 Years as a Multi-Media Whore* (San Francisco: Cleis Press, 1991), 160.
[10] We should not forget that similar femme-inistic positions and taboo breaches existed well before queer or post-pornographic conceptualizations. Daschner would therefore certainly fit the tradition of someone like Anita Berber (1899–1928) for example.
[11] Margarita Tsomou, *Femme-Praktiken. Wer hat Angst vor Weiblichkeit?* [Femme practices. Who's afraid of femininity?], *Hugs and Kisses*, issue 3 (April 2010).
[12] The concept of female masculinity refers back to the book by American queer theorist Jack Halberstam in particular, which is now an integral part of the queer canon. Jack Halberstam, *Female Masculinity* (Durham: Duke University Press, 1998).
[13] Sabine Fuchs, *Femme! radikal—queer—feminin* (Berlin: Querverlag, 2009), 18.

the queer scene, summon up the courage to reference themselves with the co-ordinates of the 'weaker sex' and therefore as feminine."[11] With the marks of femininity the femme signals a paradox: the queers and feminists who believed that the only way to resist the heterosexual matrix is to reject the feminine and turn the biological reference "woman = feminine" into its opposite (as the butch does when performing her female masculinity)[12] have not only often ignored but also underestimated the femme. At worst she is even denounced as forever suspect because of the fact that in everyday life she would pass as an apparently heterosexual woman. As Sabine Fuchs writes in *Femme! radikal—queer—feminin*: "While the motto for most lesbians is 'resistance to femininity', for femmes it could be 'resistance through femininity'."[13] And yet the femme does not naturalize gender; rather, she uses the artificial performance technologies of eye-shadow and nail polish, lipstick and high heels as a specifically queer/femme-inistic weapon that makes use of the feminine masquerade in the same way as a spy uses their fake passport. Here the artefacts installed on her body, which previously had been invested as the markings of submissive women stereotypes such as the wife or even the whore (think only of the corset), are freed of their stigmatization. [...]

[In *Flaming Flamingos,*] anyone paying close attention will already have spotted the artist among the ranks of the chorus at the start of the film, where she has assumed an egalitarian place as part of the social queer structure. Here we see that Katrina Daschner does not see her role as endlessly hogging the limelight on stage, diva-like. Her work is that of affecting the character of the queer space, a ritual which ultimately seeks to cancel out the dualism of representation and quantity. While the stage dances on without her, the entire chorus has been infected with femininity by the vector of numerous long-haired wigs—a situation as eerie as it is utopian. Endless smooching and snogging ensues among the members of the chorus; the queer urges and desires invoked by Daschner and her dance have finally spread to the crowd.

Her work is done. The oeuvre is complete.

Salon Lady Chutney

Salon Lady Chutney (2001–2002) was an artist-run performance space by Katrina Daschner, Johanna Kirsch, and Stefanie Seibold. The setting of the salon itself was a stage, a bar, and an exhibition space in a former hair salon. Each week, the salon was filled to the brim, for, at the time, there were no comparable performance places for exchange in Vienna, and venues had yet to be established. A flourishing network of mostly queer artists and theorists working on performative and performance practices ultimately developed.

FRISEUR JULIE

Salon Lady Chutney
ANGE

Salon Lady Chutney

SV DAMENKRAFT

SV DAMENKRAFT (2003–2008) was a band established by Katrina Daschner, Sabine Marte, Gin Müller, and Christina Nemec. Their common language was agit-queer à la FEMPLOITATION, composed of minimal-brute Tech-Lektro-Punk-Pop and explicitly sexualized choreographies as well as poetic activistic texts and glamorous stylings.

CLUB BURLESQUE BRUTAL

CLUB BURLESQUE BRUTAL (2009–2014) was hosted by Katrina Daschner and presented contributions from various queer performers. CBB presented bizarre, glamorous, intelligent, and extremely funny burlesque shows, mostly at brut Wien. Daschner, as Frau Professor la Rose, led the nights with her unmistakable moderations on a range from almost embarrassed to extremely explicit and quite pointed.

The overall motto was:
More is more and less is just less!

TEACH ME A LESSON

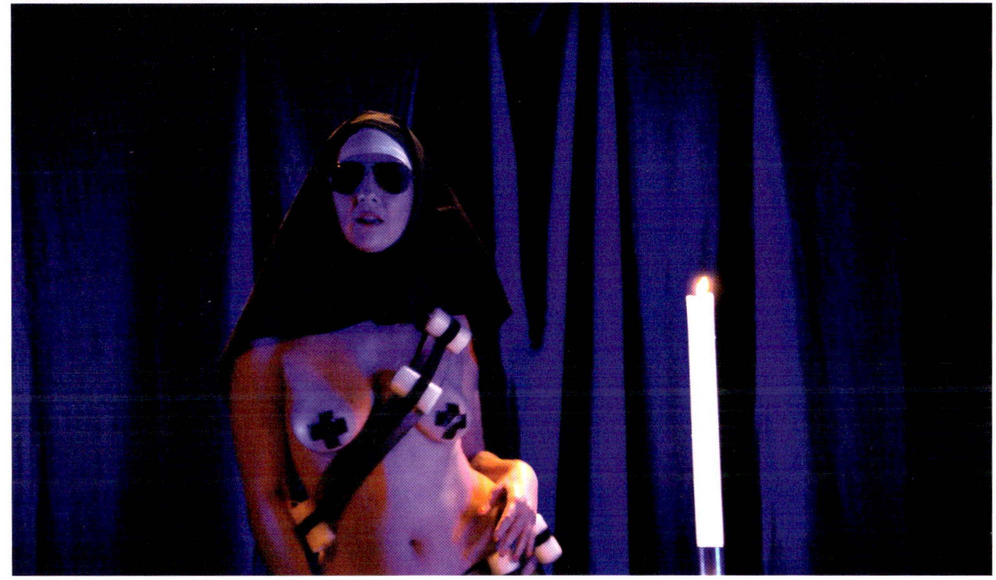

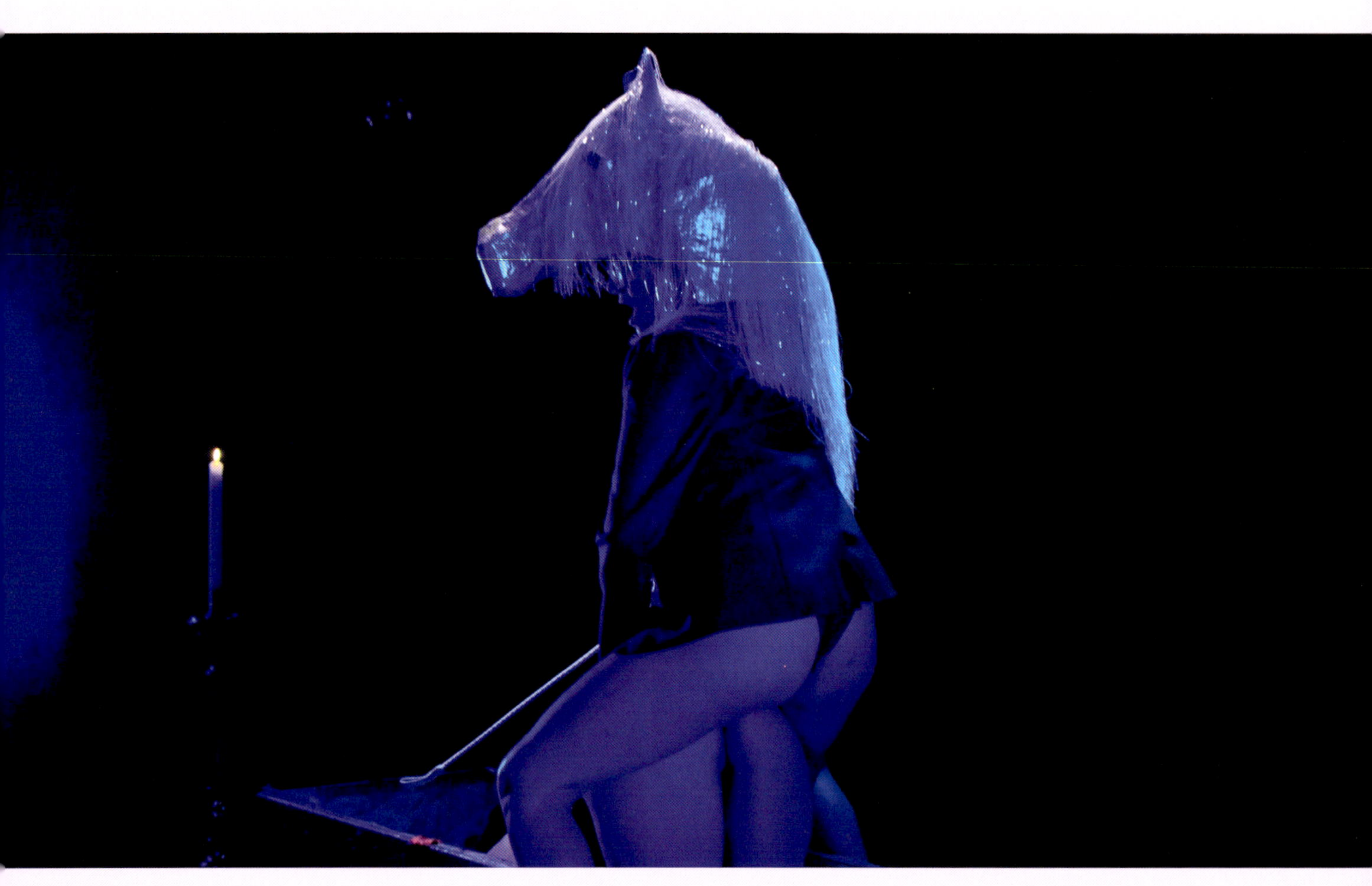

Show

Katrina Daschner's solo exhibition "BURN & GLOOM! GLOW & MOON! Thousand Years of Troubled Genders" took place at Kunsthalle Wien from June 30 to October 23, 2022.

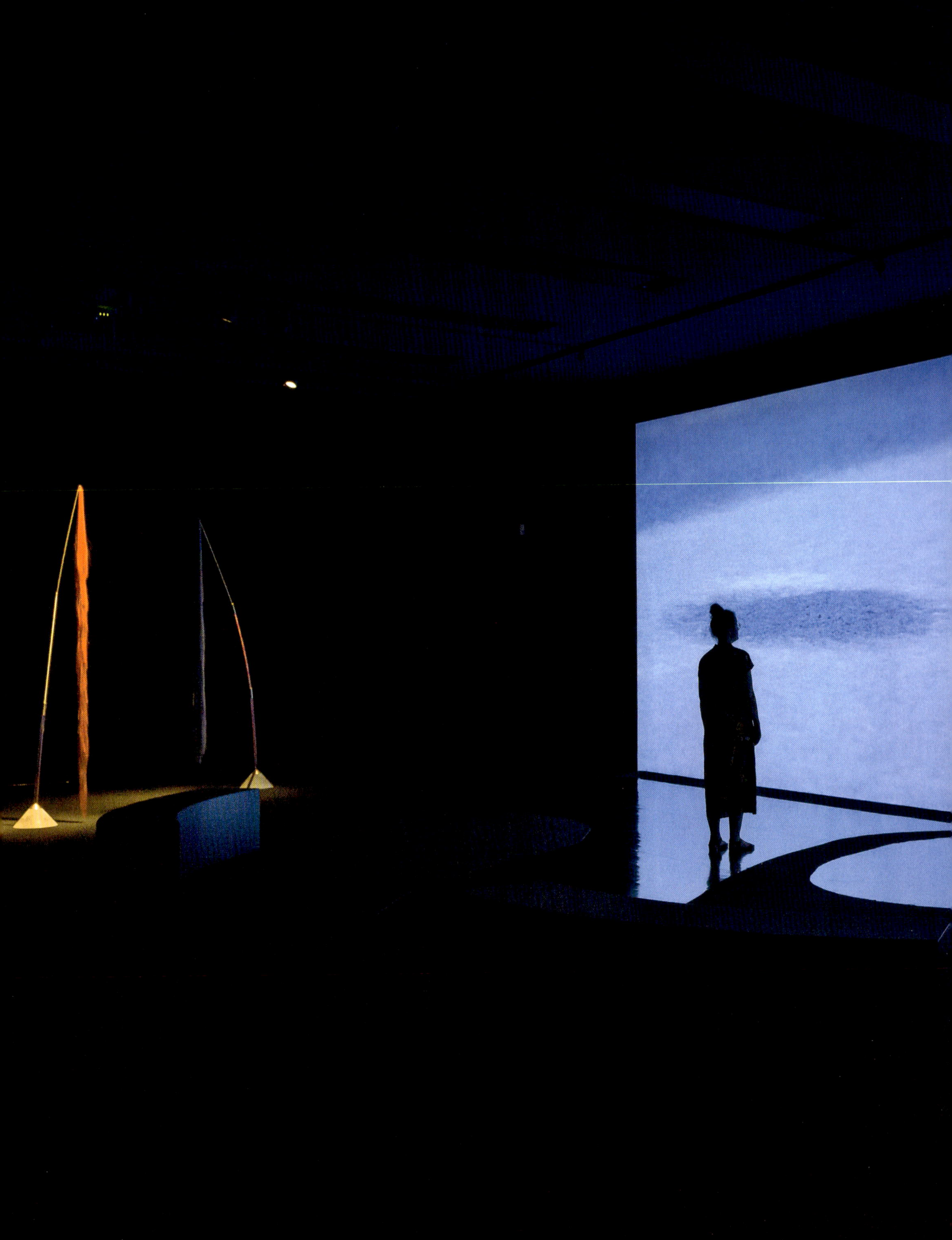

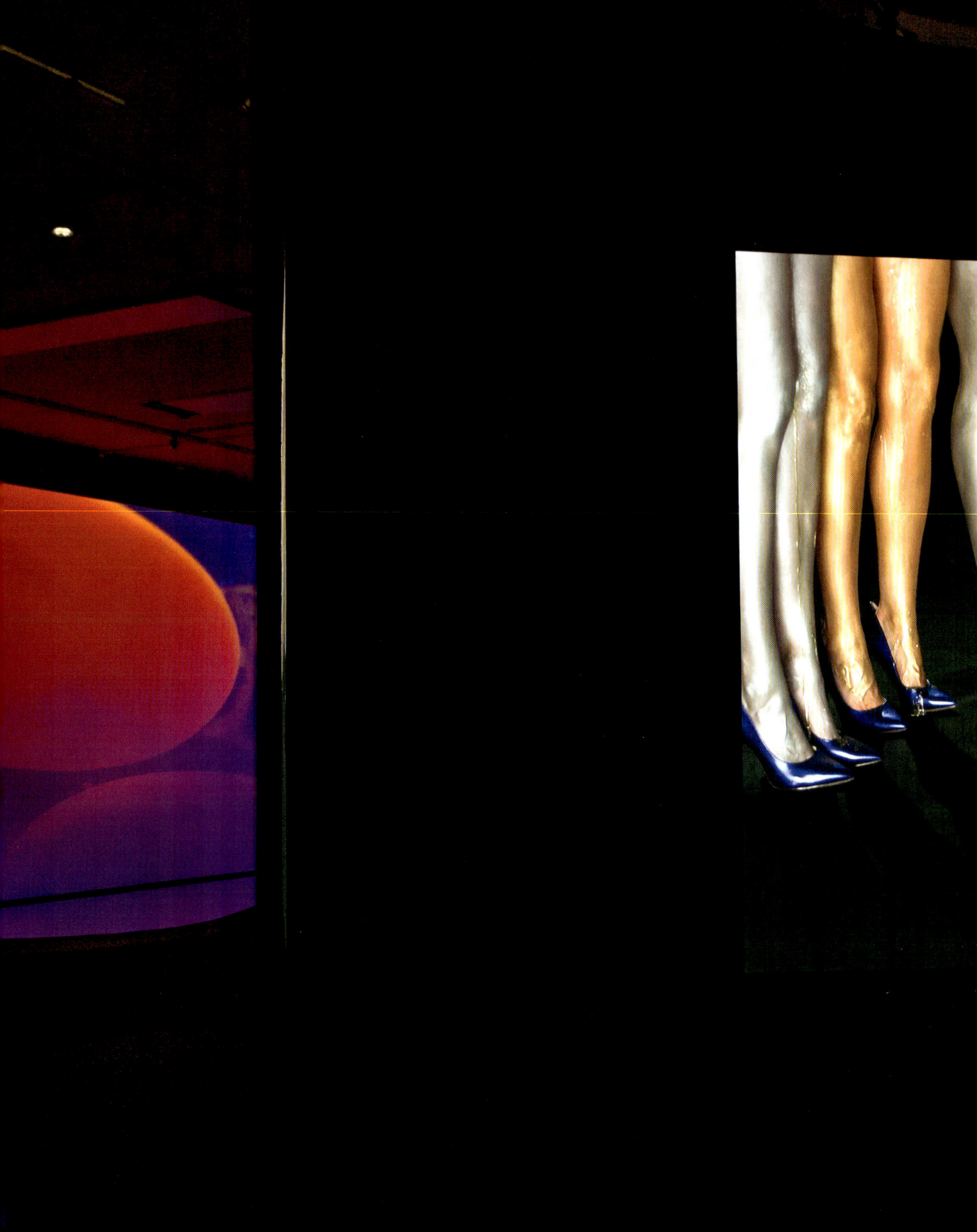

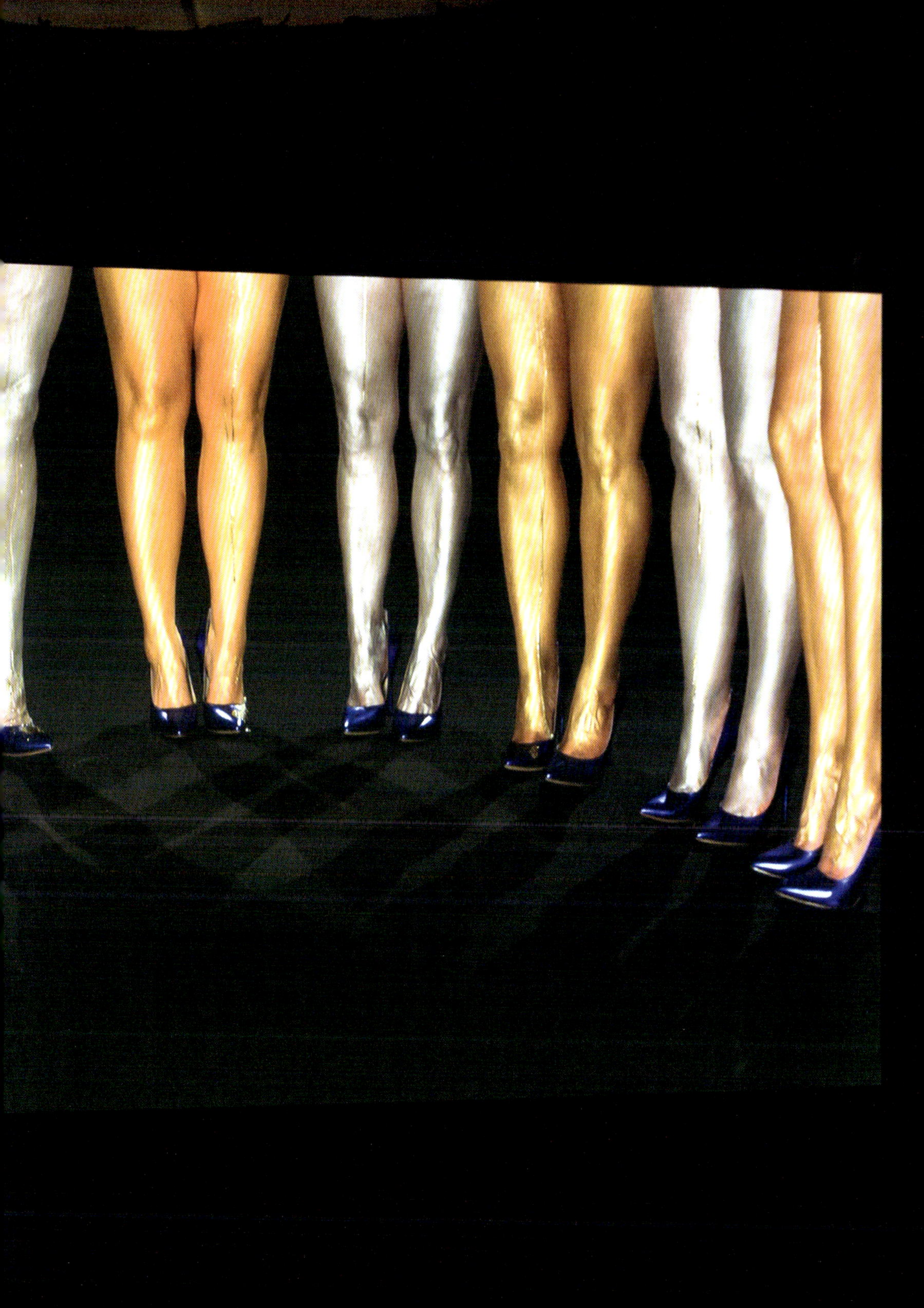

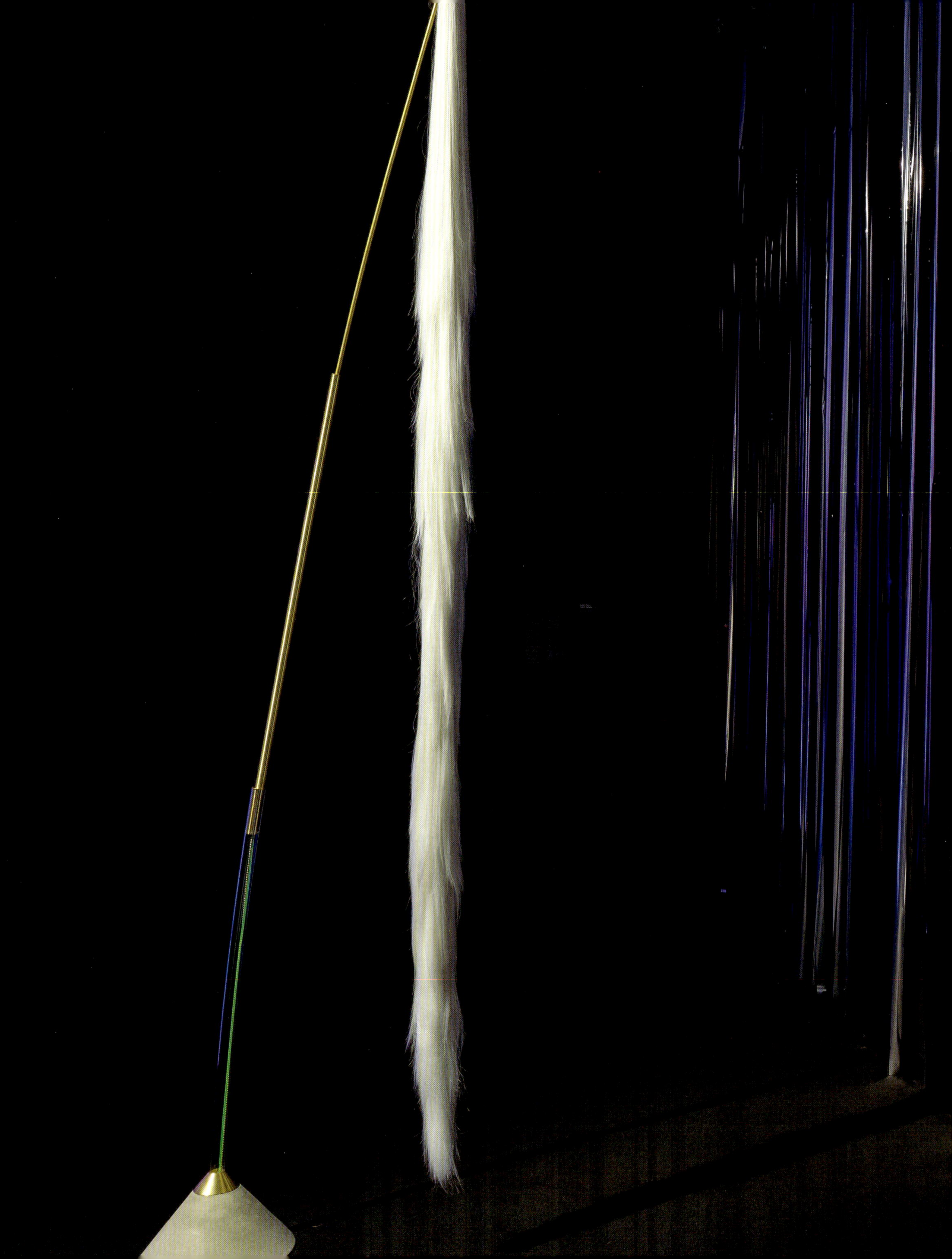

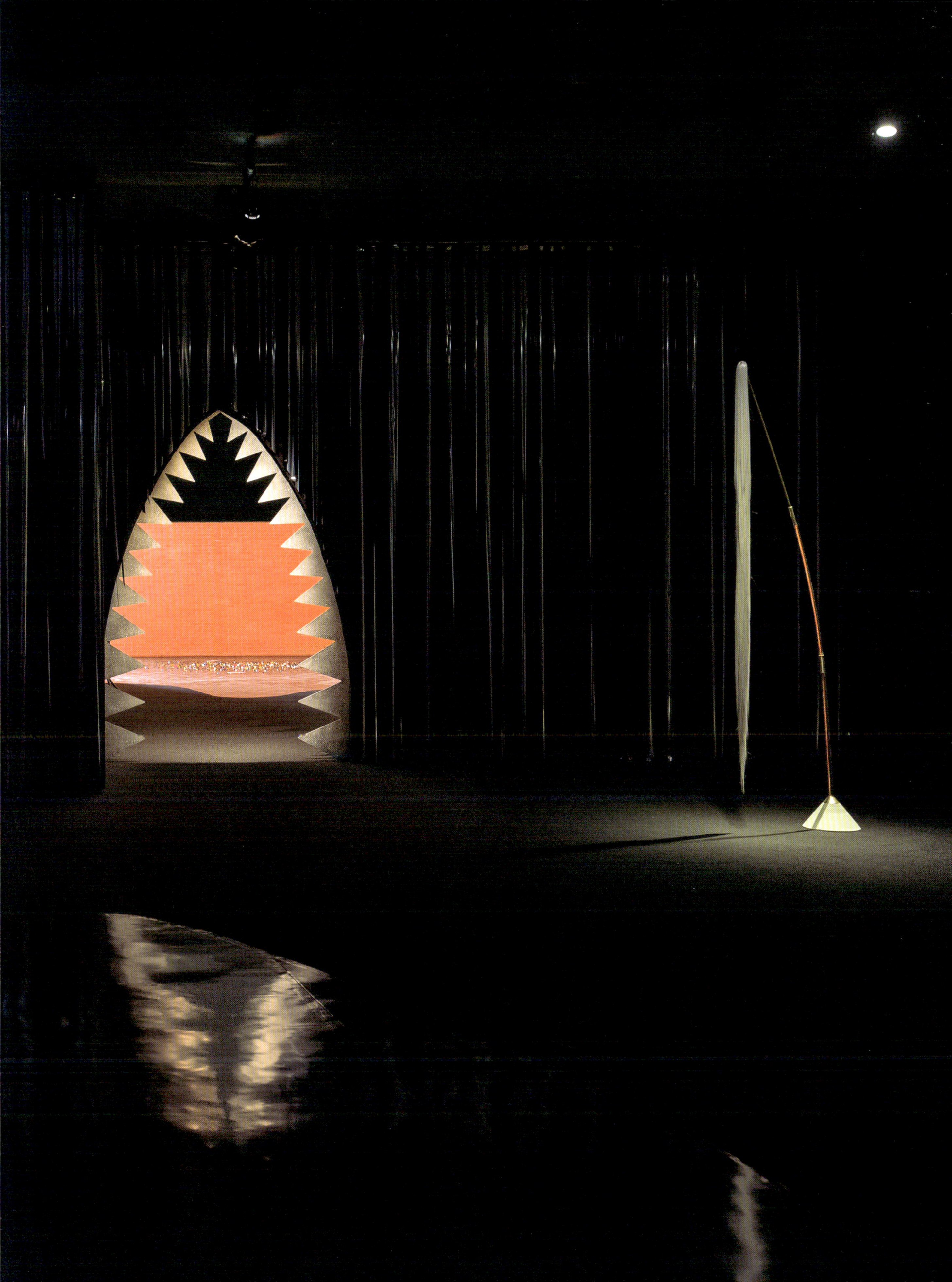

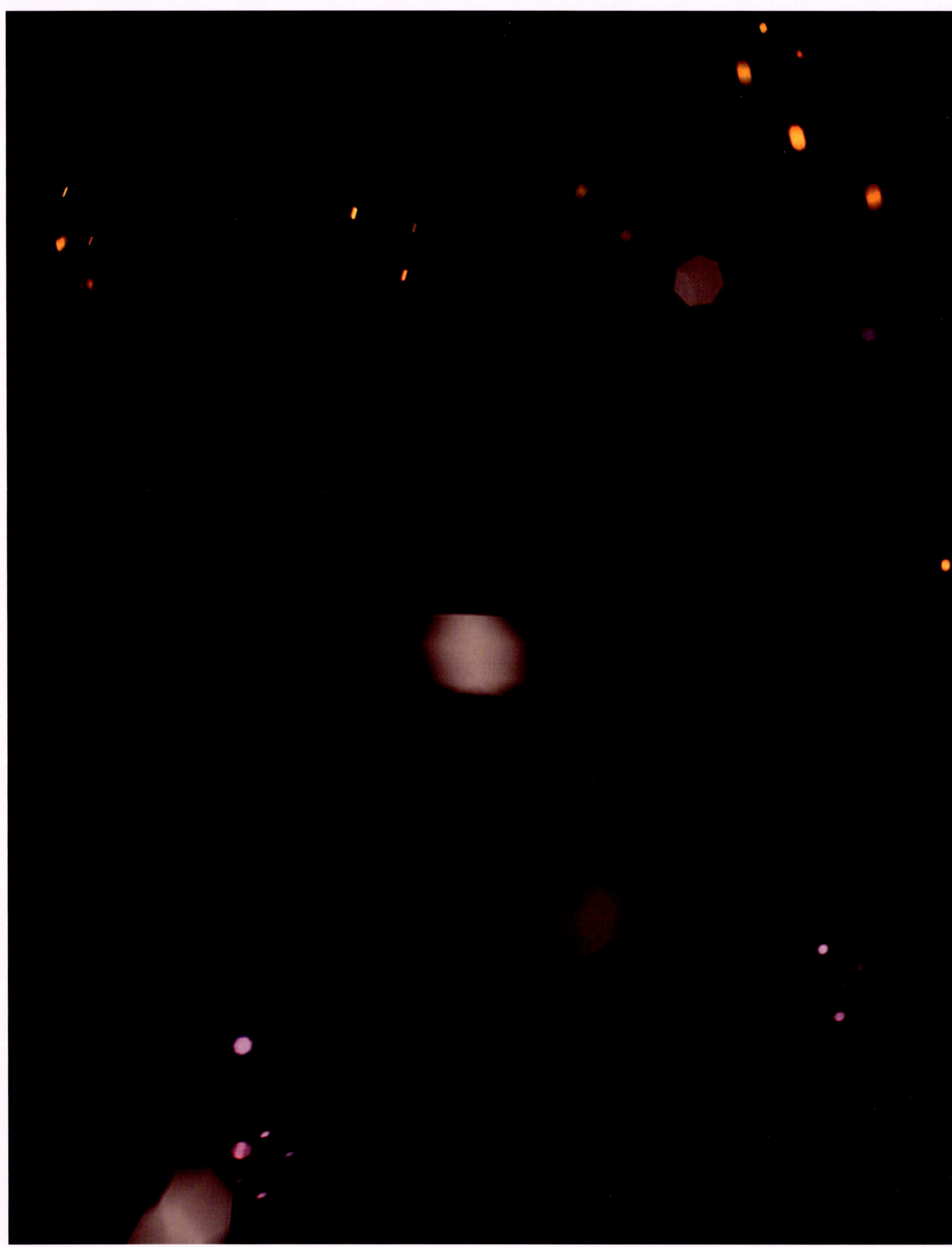

Films

Hiding in the Lights

Shimmering Opacity and the Glitter Commons in the Work of Katrina Daschner

Essay by
Amelia Groom

If you were there at the right time, a shower of rainbow glitter confetti may have fallen onto you as you arrived at Katrina Daschner's exhibition "BURN & GLOOM! GLOW & MOON! Thousand Years of Troubled Genders." For her work *Basic Stage (Collective Energy)* (2022), the artist set up an overhead mechanical contraption at the entrance to Kunsthalle Wien, programming it to release a bucket of sparkles every thirty minutes. As with many of the new sculptural installation works in the exhibition, this rain of glitter is something that can be traced back to the artist's films from the last decade or so. *Hiding in the Lights* (2013), for instance—the second of Daschner's eight-part short film series of the same name—opens with metallic silver confetti flittering in the air as it falls from above. In fact, right throughout Daschner's moving image works, there are things that sparkle and shine: sequins, diamantés, throbbing lights on shimmering makeup, metallic golden piss streaming down legs painted pearlescent in silver and gold, nipples adorned in twinkling jewels, sea creatures with tendrils that pulse and glow, pearls, champagne, lots of gleam, gloss, glamour, glitz, and glitter.

Glitter: it's fabulous, it's cheap, it's vulgar and glamorous, tacky and communal, iridescent and evanescent, sexy and non-linear. It's unmappable; it gets everywhere. It's the surface of the sea in the early morning sun; it's the stars above in the night sky. It's a tiny little galaxy worn on your cheek; and it's deeply queer. Like the rainbow, glitter has long been linked with LGBTQ+ aesthetics and politics. It sparkles through the histories of queer nightlife and performance art, including the intersecting worlds of drag, burlesque, vaudeville, and cabaret (aesthetic legacies with which Daschner's work is entangled). And it flashes up in queer protest tactics—including "glitter bombing," in which activists shower queerphobic politicians and organizations in this sticky substance that stands for the lives they despise.[1]

In 2011, Minnesota activist Nick Espinosa went to an event hosted by an anti-gay organization, where Newt Gingrich (a conservative politician who later became a key Trump ally) was signing copies of his book. When Espinosa got to the front of the line, he doused Gingrich in a rain of sparkles while shouting, "Feel the rainbow, Newt! Stop the hate! Stop anti-gay politics!" Video documentation of the event shows Gingrich and his wife awkwardly trying to brush the glitter off the table, and off themselves, while continuing to sign books as if nothing has happened; as if they weren't sitting in the middle of this beautiful, unmanageable mess of sparkles; as if it's possible to ignore glitter.[2]

A glitter-based insistence on unapologetic queer visibility can also be traced in Glitter + Ash, a campaign by Parity, a New York–based Christian LGBTQ+ organization. Since 2017, Parity has promoted blending purple sparkles with blessed Ash Wednesday ashes so that the crosses on people's foreheads can make queer life within the church fabulously conspicuous. "WE WILL BE SEEN. Glitter is like love. It's irresistible and irrepressible," reads a statement on their website. "Glitter is an inextricable element of queer history. It is how we have displayed our gritty, scandalous hope. We make ourselves fabulously conspicuous, giving offense to the arbiters of respectability that allow coercive power to flourish."[3]

In their shimmering autobiographical essay "The Queer Voice: Reparative Poetry Rituals & Glitter Perversions" (2015), the poet CAConrad writes about being "unexpectedly liberated" in high school when they were outed as "a faggot queer" by the other kids. "I no longer needed to play by the rules of normal people because I had been kicked out of acceptable society," they recall. "I raised my hand to the mirror and vowed to never apologize for my love of glitter. The day after being Outed, purple and orange glitter appeared on my notebooks and eyebrows, glitter was my sacred shield as the other kids referred to me as Faggot so often they seemed to forget my real name." CAConrad advises everyone to "keep it in your shirt pocket in case you walk by a very sad place, then sprinkle a little red and purple with a touch of gold." "Glitter," they write,

> "is not enabling denial of the world's pain but instead helps us endure the bleak results of those who are in denial of how we need one another. If you have a scar or bent nose that has become the center of your life trust me when I say own it and apply glitter blush directly, immediately. Before you die join me in loving our flesh, loving our lives."[4]

*

While glitter claims space and demands attention, its relationship to visibility is far from straightforward. It's in your face and over the top, but its effect is always elusive: through its granular scintillation, it takes the light and breaks it up, refracting it out in multiple directions. To look at glitter is to look at tiny points of momentary focus that flash up as quickly as they withdraw. Glitter winks at you. Its visual field is fragmentary and full of movement—you're facing a multiplicity of locations where differentiation is always unstable. Glitter says, "look at me," as it catches the light with bright bursts, but it also says, "what you're looking at cannot be pinned down." Remember that the word "glamour" comes from the Scottish gramarye, relating to magic, illusion, enchantment, and sorcery: "to cast the glamour" was to cast a spell that deceived the eyes and made things appear to change into other things—or to disappear completely.[5]

Daschner's work speaks to the politics of queer in/visibility through an aesthetic of glittery opacity. Her *Hiding in the Lights* films are glittery not only in their frequent inclusion of shimmering substances but also in their glittery energy; through their emphasis on change, metamorphosis, and fragmentary imagery that can flitter into the light and then vanish again. In *Plum Circus* (2019), for instance, there's someone in red lipstick taking a bath in a red liquid. She pours the liquid over her face and chest. It's like blood and red wine, and then, all of a sudden, it's red and silver glitter that she's pouring over her tits. In *Parole Rosette* (2012), the first film in the series, someone bends over while a gloved hand ceremonially unzips a "window" at the back of her pants so that her ass cheeks become fully exposed. The camera briefly cuts away to a close-up of the crack between two red velvet seats in a theatre: an ass discovered in the furniture. Then the camera cuts back to the bare human ass, only now it's covered in shimmering violet glitter, and there's a velvety red rose planted in the crack. The editing constructs an erotics of transformation—with shapeshifting alterations that glitter in and out of each other, with no final resting places.

Glitter looks best at night—as with the stars above, which are invisible in the daytime, its iridescence is given form by darkness. Visitors to "BURN & GLOOM! GLOW & MOON!" entered the main exhibition space through the passageway of a giant vagina dentata with pearlescent silver teeth. On the other side, they found themselves in a space so dim that it took several minutes for the retina to adjust. Throughout the exhibition, there was a constant interplay of light and darkness; sparkly and reflective surfaces would gleam in the flick of light inside this very nocturnal atmosphere. Foiled silver curtains mirroring and mirrored in the pools of high-gloss flooring installed throughout the space; films that glittered with multifaceted shimmers projected above shiny grounds, which reflected their fleeting lights. Many lights, but always the possibility of "hiding in the light."

In the 1970s, Roland Barthes turned to shimmers as spaces of nuance that outplay the paradigms of dialectical and binary thinking—shimmer as a site of tiny, twinkling gradations and changes, which "substitutes for the idea of opposition that of the slight difference, of the onset, of the effort toward difference."[6] This read on shimmer has been picked up in more recent years within queer and trans studies, including Eliza Steinbock's work on "shimmering images" and the aesthetics of change in trans cinema.[7] Characterizing trans ontologies as process-oriented rather than object-oriented, Steinbock draws from Barthes's observation that the shimmering object is one "whose aspect, perhaps whose meaning, is subtly modified according to the angle of the subject's gaze."[8]

The appearance of glitter depends on the viewer's perspective. It's like anamorphosis, where the image that flashes up for a specific vantage point doesn't appear at all when looked at from other angles. Holbein's anamorphic skull shows itself only when you stand in a certain position, and glitter only sparkles when the refracted light fleetingly aligns with your gaze. As you move, it moves; and its movements also move you. There's something very queer in this mode of visuality, if we think about the brilliantly inventive practices of desire that have necessarily circulated through code, subtext and subterfuge—always being attuned to the meaning that emerges from situated context, never needing to aim for a totalized, universalizing field of visibility.

Against the predatory enlightenment regime of the visual that separates the viewing subject from the immobilized object of their gaze, this is an invitation to understand perception and knowledge as embodied, situated, partial, and relational. Glitter emerges in relationality; for this reason, much is lost in the documentation that exists of Daschner's kinetic work *Basic Stage (Collective Energy)*. Lens-based representations of glitter do not themselves sparkle. Rather than partaking in a dynamic relationship of refracted light that is broken up and sent into the scatter of fleeting appearances, documentational photographs flatten the visual field with a unified vantage point and static representational logic.

*

At one point in CAConrad's autobiographical essay about their "glitter perversions," they imagine joining a Glitter Cult devoted to Henry Ruschmann, the farmer who invented modern glitter in New Jersey in 1934. "There would be a very shiny commune for us with edible glitter in every cocktail and plate of food, glitter flowing through us at all times," they write. "After

[1] For a history of glitter bombing as a queer protest tactic, see Anya M. Galli Robertson, "Mixing glitter and protest to support LGBTQ rights," *The Conversation*, March 12, 2017, https://theconversation.com/mixing-glitter-and-protest-to-support-lgbtq-rights-74026 and Anya M. Galli, "How Glitter Bombing Lost Its Sparkle: The Emergence and Decline of a Novel Social Movement Tactic," *Mobilization: An International Quarterly 21*, no. 3 (September 2016): 259–81, https://doi.org/10.17813/1086-671X-20-3-259.
[2] "Raw Video: Gingrich Hit With Glitter in Minn.," *Associated Press*, May 17, 2011, video, 1:18, https://youtu.be/LSb3kTA6vVI. The impossibility of ignoring glitter was also key in the *revolución diamantina* ("glitter revolution") that emerged in Mexico City in 2019, with women throwing masses of pink glitter while protesting rape culture and rising femicide in Mexico. The feminist illustrator Mariana "Maremoto" Lorenzo Contreras remarked at the time, "During the march, we threw glitter at people watching us, we threw it everywhere. We wanted to leave a pink stain on the street. We want the violence that we experience as women in this country to be like glitter: impossible to ignore." See Lauren Cocking, "The History of Using Glitter As a Symbol of Protest," *Teen Vogue*, August 28, 2019, www.teenvogue.com/story/mexico-protest-glitter-explainer.
[3] "Glitter Ash Wednesday," Parity, https://parity.nyc/order-glitter-ash-2021.
[4] CAConrad, "The Queer Voice: Reparative Poetry Rituals & Glitter Perversions," *Poetry Foundation*, June 22, 2015, www.poetryfoundation.org/harriet-books/2015/06/the-queer-voice-reparative-poetry-rituals-glitter-perversions. See also CAConrad's poem "Glitter in My Wounds," in which they write, "glitter on a queer is not to dazzle but to / unsettle the foundation of this murderous culture." "Glitter in My Wounds," *Poetry* (November 2018), www.poetryfoundation.org/poetrymagazine/poems/148106/glitter-in-my-wounds.
[5] *Gramarye* was also related to scholarship and craft—in the occult sense, but also more generally; the word "grammar" is etymologically linked to the word "glamour" in this sense. Reflecting on her time as a

a night of prodigious glitter ingestion the toilets at The Ruschmann Temple would sparkle like no other toilets; the dirtier they get the more glamorous they become." Later in the essay, CAConrad proposes a new invention: "A product in power bar form or delicious milkshake that turns his semen to glitter jizz, and we coat each other's faces with it then go to the club. You just know it will be the new rage! The DJ will turn on his black light and everyone will scream with joy as faces glow turquoise, green, pink, and red from glitter jizz!"

In both of these hilarious scenarios, glitter is a technology of transcorporeality; it flows through, out of, and across bodies, sweeping them up into a dazzling form of collectivity. Throughout Daschner's "BURN & GLOOM! GLOW & MOON!," there were tributes to the collaborators and friends who have been a part of the artist's practice for decades. Lining the walls of the Kunsthalle's foyer space, for instance, was a prominent mural showing a still from Daschner's film *Flaming Flamingos* (2011) (the third part of her early film trilogy *NOUVELLE BURLESQUE BRUTAL*), in which the artist appears as a body within a group of bodies. The film features an extended silent shot of glittery silver confetti falling against a black background before cutting to this group figuration of intergenerational queer sociality. Everyone is dressed in red and black. We cannot tell who is who. They're standing very close to each other —some are kissing or caressing—and they're all wearing long wigs that cover their faces. Deindividualized, they form a writhing mass, an ensemble body where everyone is feeling and holding each other.

"BURN & GLOOM! GLOW & MOON!" brought together works by Daschner from the 1990s up until the present. Her earliest works were experimental photocollage self-portraits that playfully refashioned her identity through various many-gendered expressions and guises. After around 2000, her practice shifted distinctly, insofar as she stopped working with her own body in isolation and moved towards more collective and collaborative processes. Speaking over the phone in September 2022, I asked the artist what precipitated this shift more than twenty years ago. Her answer was surprisingly succinct. "I came out," she said.[9] Coming out was not just about revealing or affirming something true about herself; it was an opening up into new forms of friendship and community. This is not a universal experience, but it is one that I —and I think many other queers—can relate to. In Daschner's case, her coming out coincided with a flourishing of community around queer performance practices; in 2001, Daschner, together with artists Stefanie Seibold and Johanna Kirsch, who was also a former partner, founded Salon Lady Chutney, an independent queer performance art space with an upstairs bar in a former hair salon in Vienna. Many of the artist's long-term collaborators were originally connected through that space, and the community that formed around the salon would come to redefine her work.

Basic Stage (Collective Energy) —Daschner's glitter shower contraption at the entrance to the exhibition—offers another tribute to her friends, although in this case, it is less figuratively representational. The title of the work holds an affirmation of the energy of collectivity, and the materiality of glitter is something that can stand for unexpected forms of community and alliance. This is the glittery commons: glitter is bad at individualized containment, it exists on an unmanageable scale, and it can remain in circulation by grabbing onto whatever and whomever comes into its orbit.[10] It seeks out cracks and crevices in bodies, objects, and spaces, and it lingers on as a sticky afterimage so that you might find telltale sparkly remnants in your bedsheets or in your belly button days after the queer party. Flashes of brilliance that hide and light up and withdraw again, hiding within the light.

copy editor for *Glamour* magazine, feminist beauty writer Autumn Whitefield-Madrano notes, "Both grammar and glamour function as a set of rules that help people articulate themselves and allow us to understand one another. I understand you are telling me of the future by the use of words like *will* and *going to*; I understand you are telling me about your vision of yourself with red lipstick and a wiggle dress." Autumn Whitefield-Madrano, "Thoughts on a Word: Glamour (Part I)," *The New Inquiry*, February 8, 2012, https://thenewinquiry.com/blog/thoughts-on-a-word-glamour-part-i.

[6] Roland Barthes, *The Neutral*, trans. Rosalind E. Krauss and Denis Hollier (New York: Columbia University Press, 2005), 51.

[7] Eliza Steinbock, *Shimmering Images: Trans Cinema, Embodiment, and the Aesthetics of Change* (Durham, NC: Duke University Press, 2019). See also Vanbasten Noronha de Araújo, "Shimmery Waste: A Queer Critique of the Narrative of Glitter Pollution" (Doctoral diss., Central European University, 2019), www.etd.ceu.edu/2019/dearaujo_vanbasten.pdf.

[8] Barthes, *The Neutral*, 51.

[9] Video call with the author, September 28, 2022.

[10] For an analysis of glitter pollution through queer and environmental lenses, see Vanbasten Noronha de Araújo, "Shimmery Waste: A Queer Critique of the Narrative of Glitter Pollution."

Parole Rosette

2012
color, silent
09:00 min

Hiding in the Lights

2013
color, sound
14:00 min

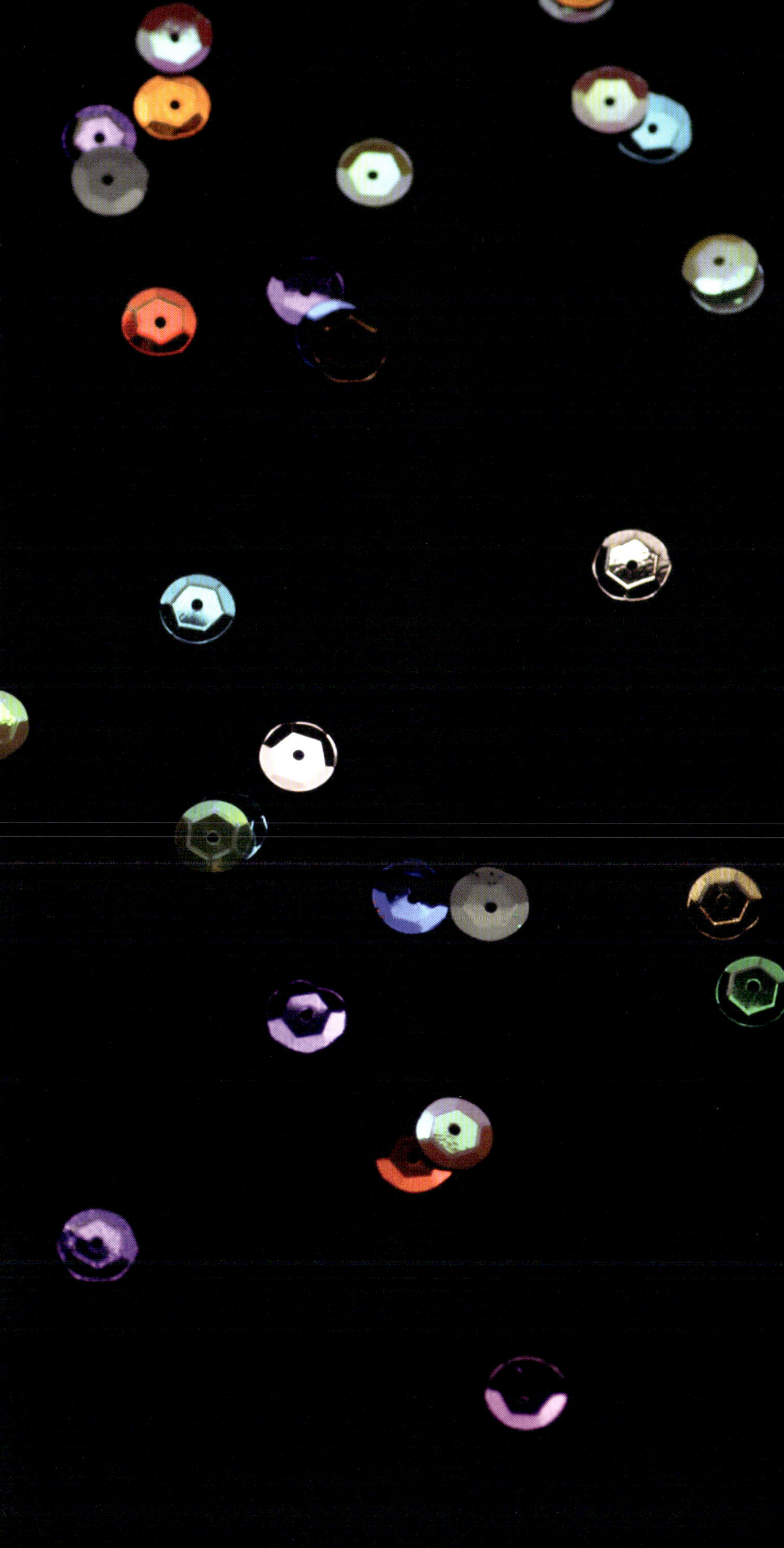

Powder Placenta

2015
color, sound
09:17 min

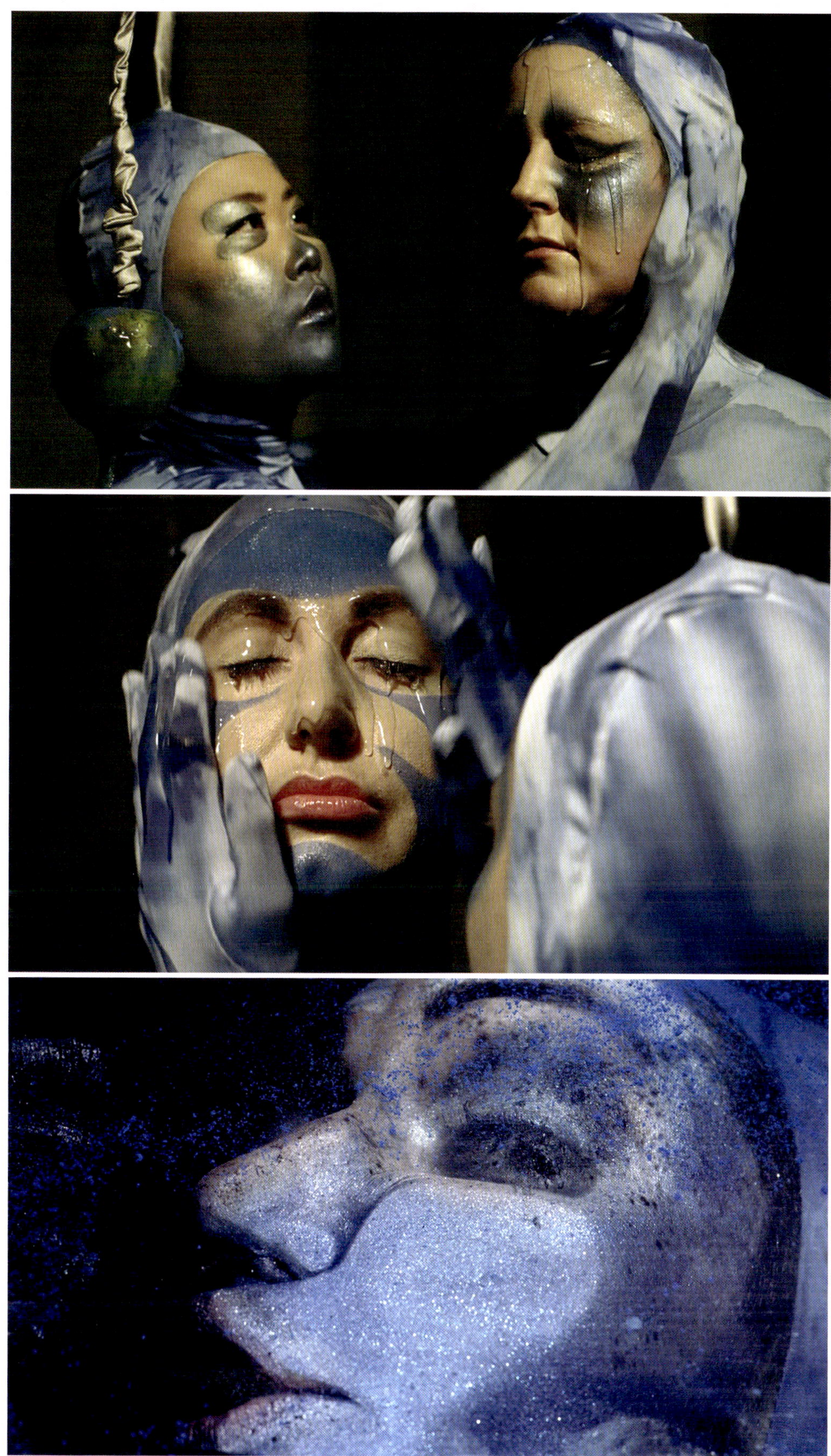

Perlenmeere

[Seas of Pearls]
2016
color, silent
08:37 min

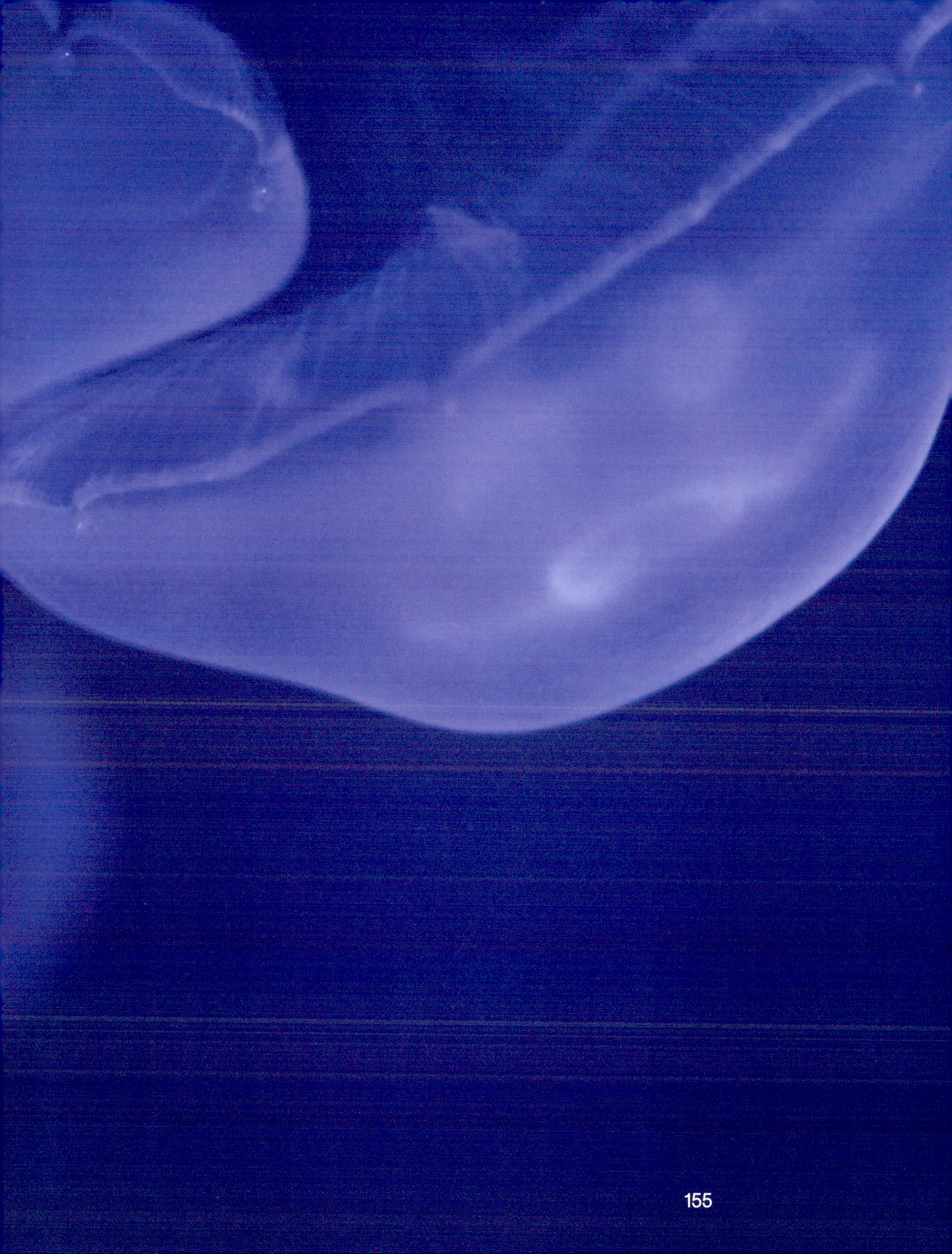

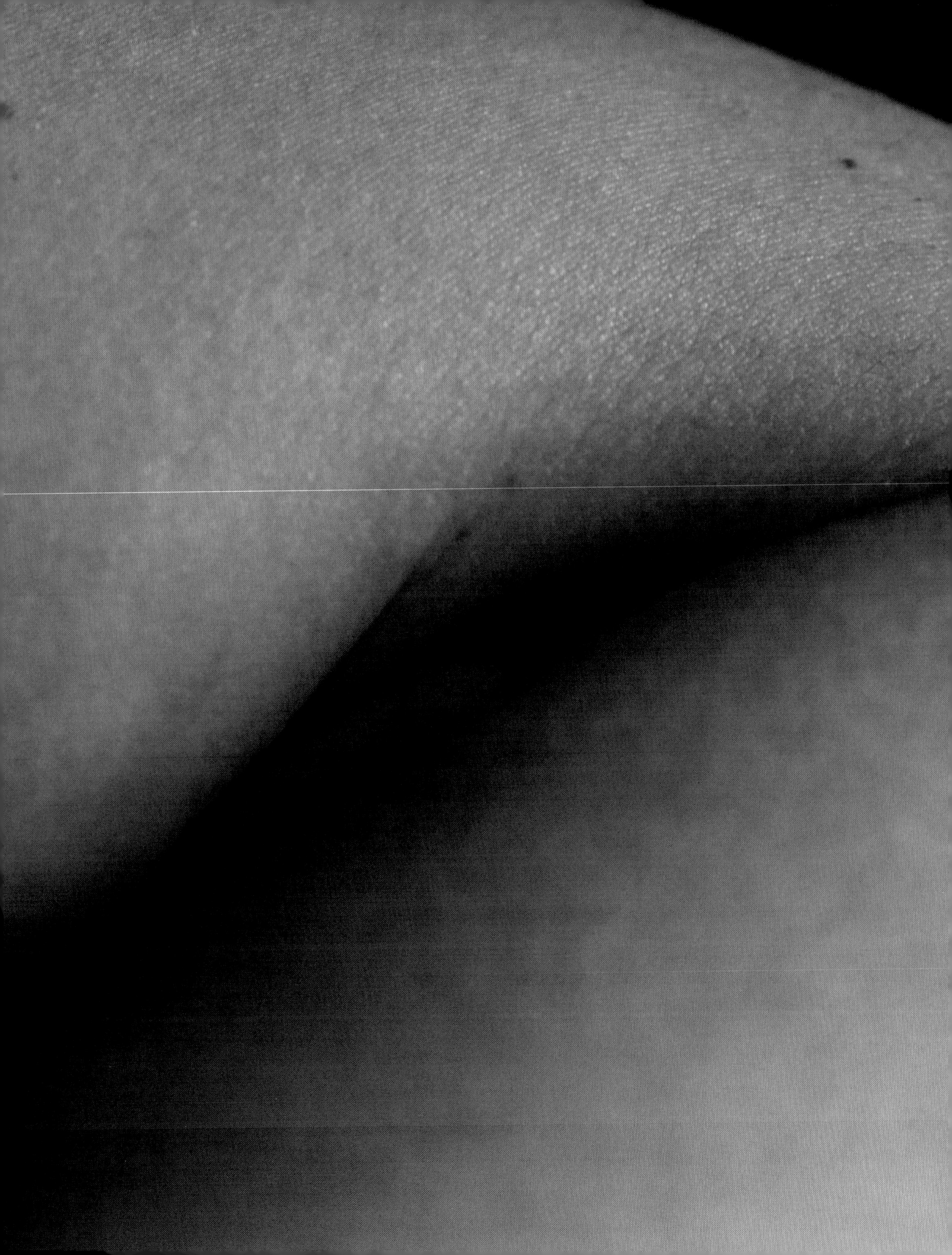

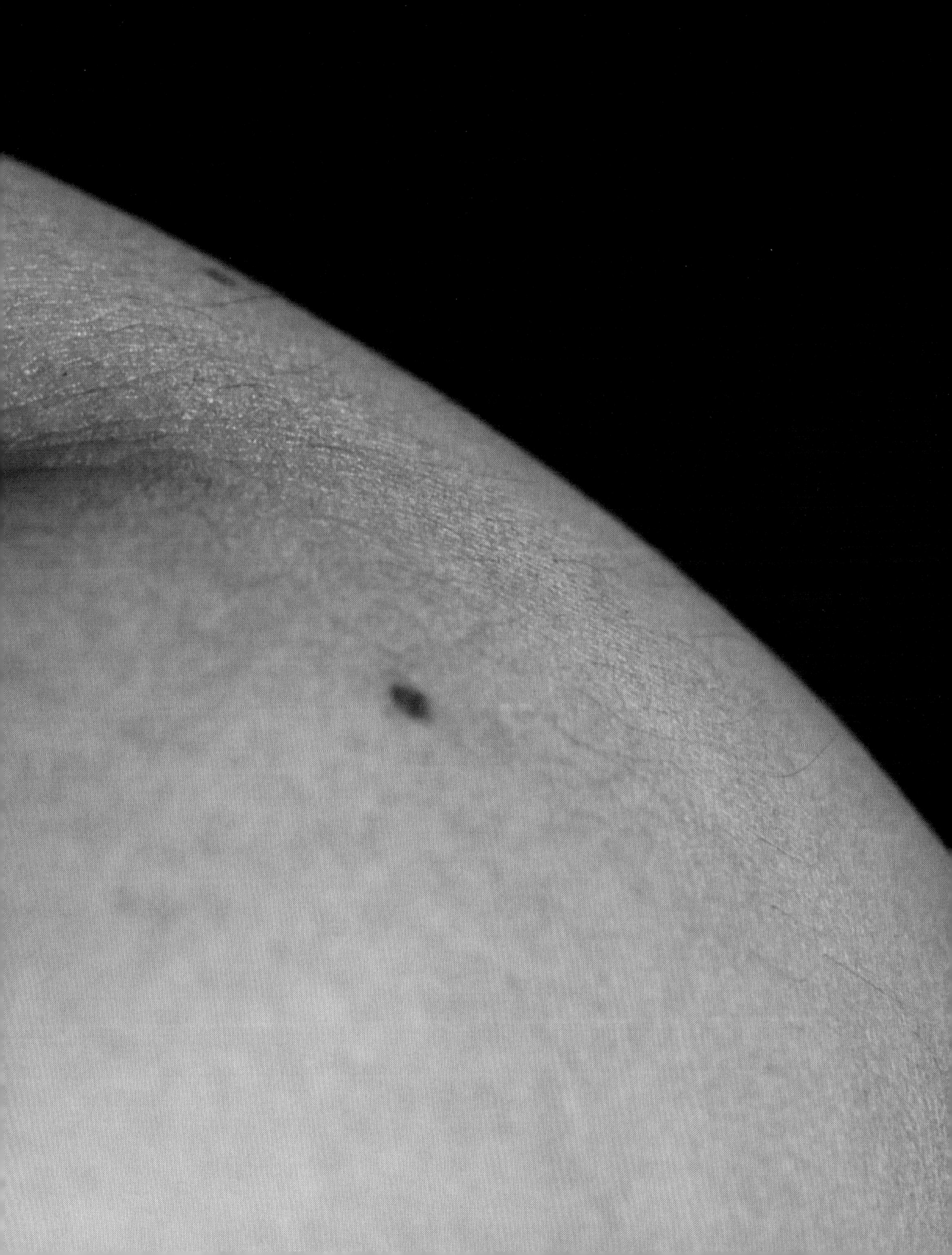

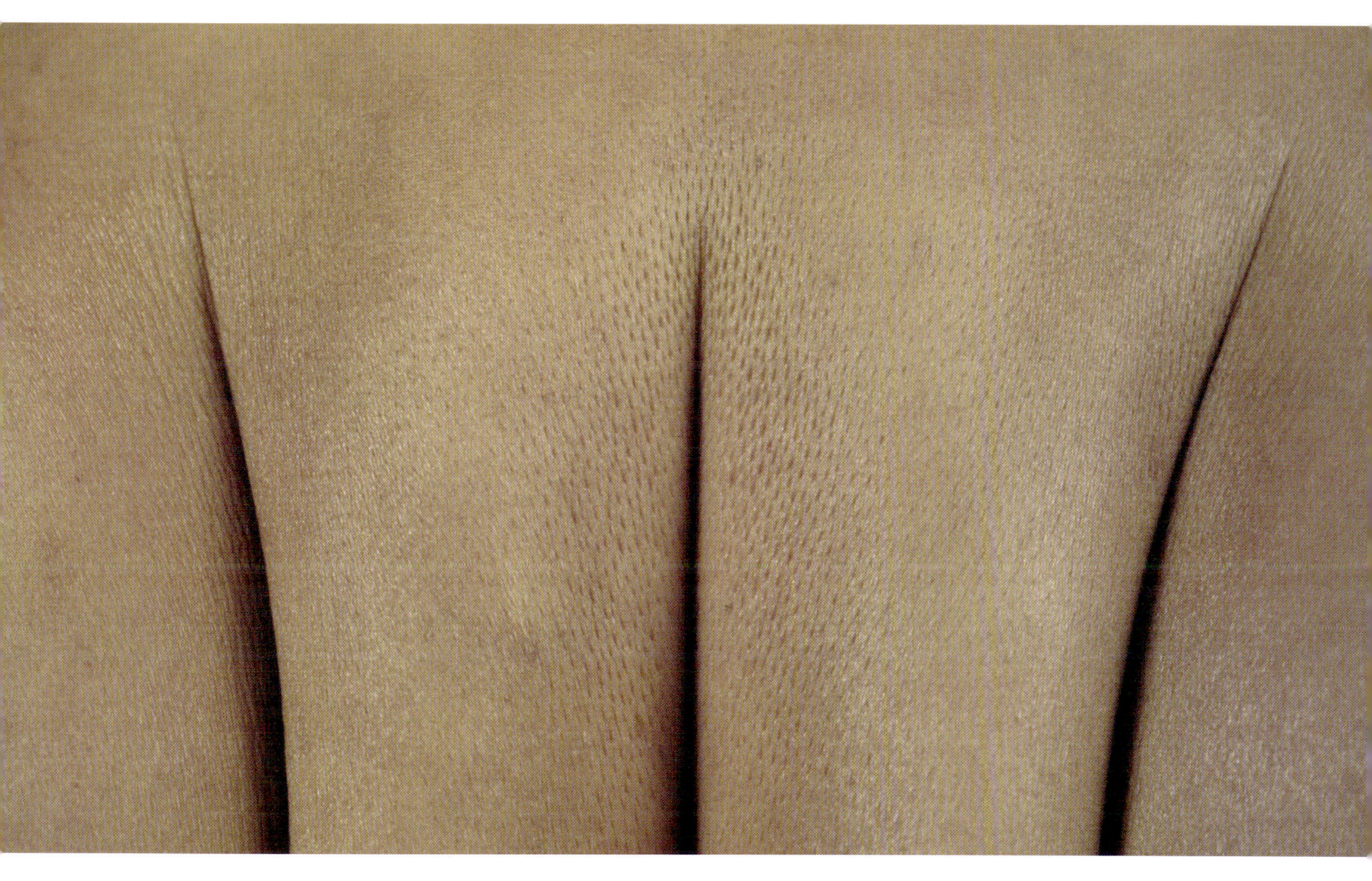

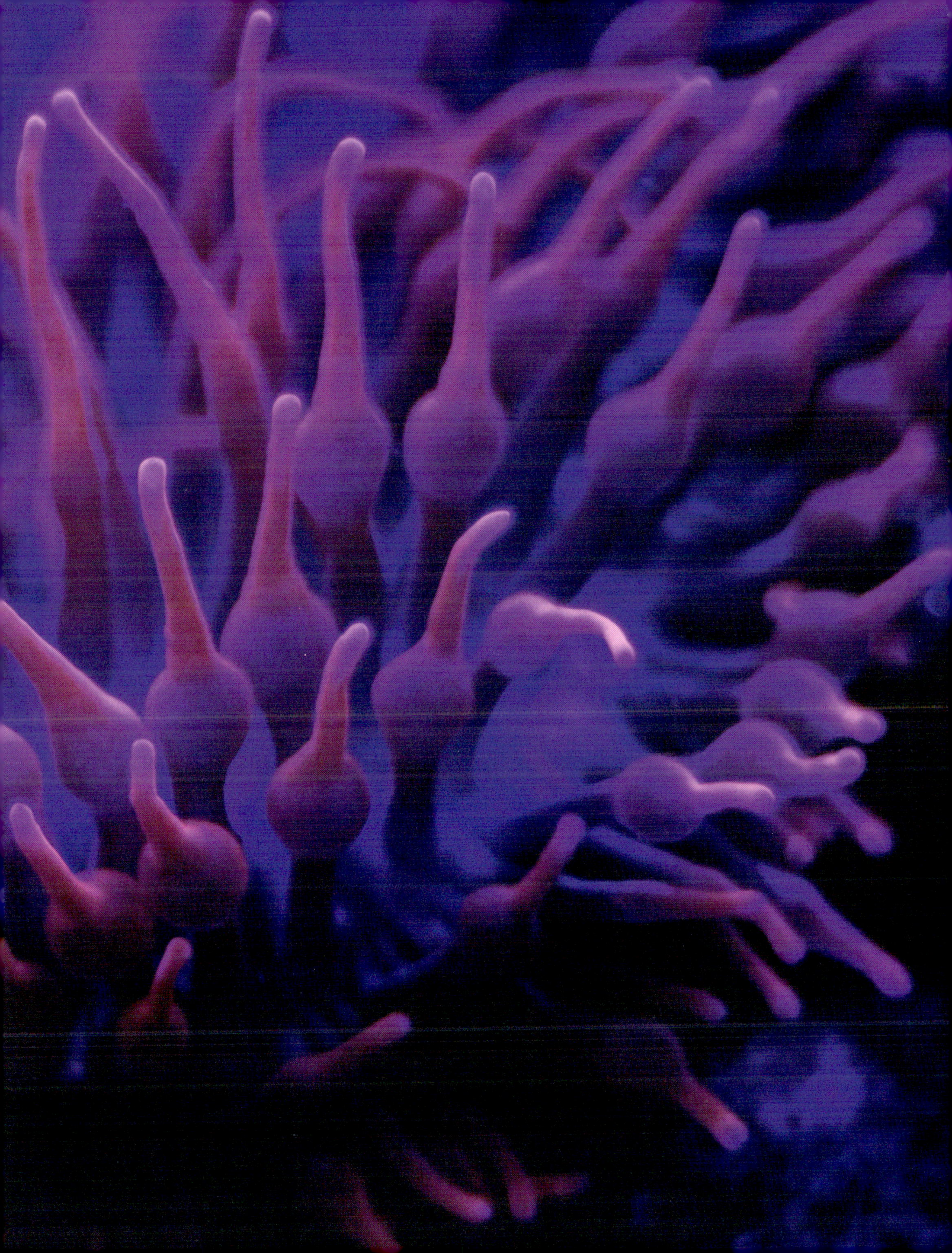

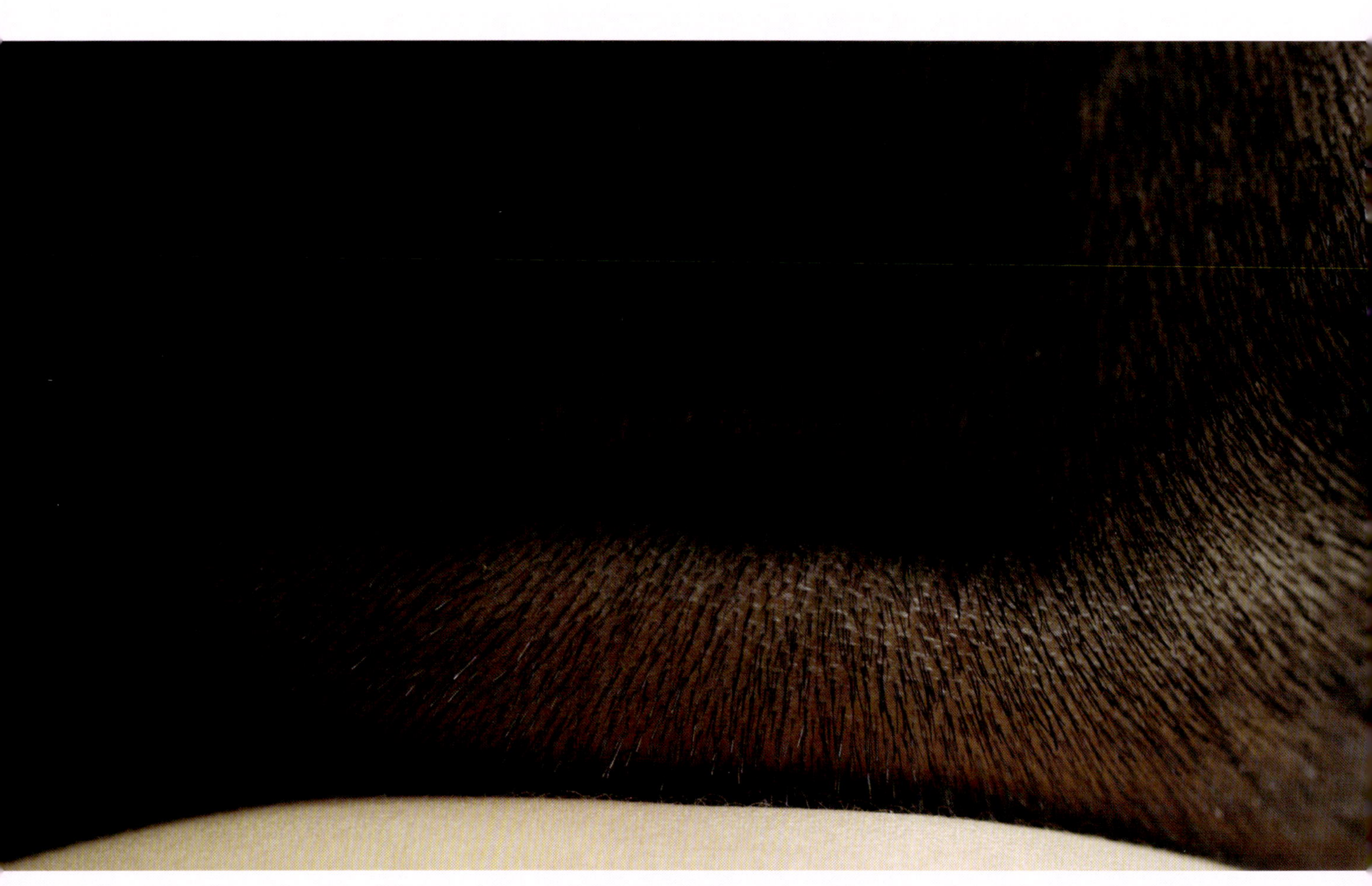

Pferdebusen

[Horse Boobs]
2017
color, sound
09:01 min

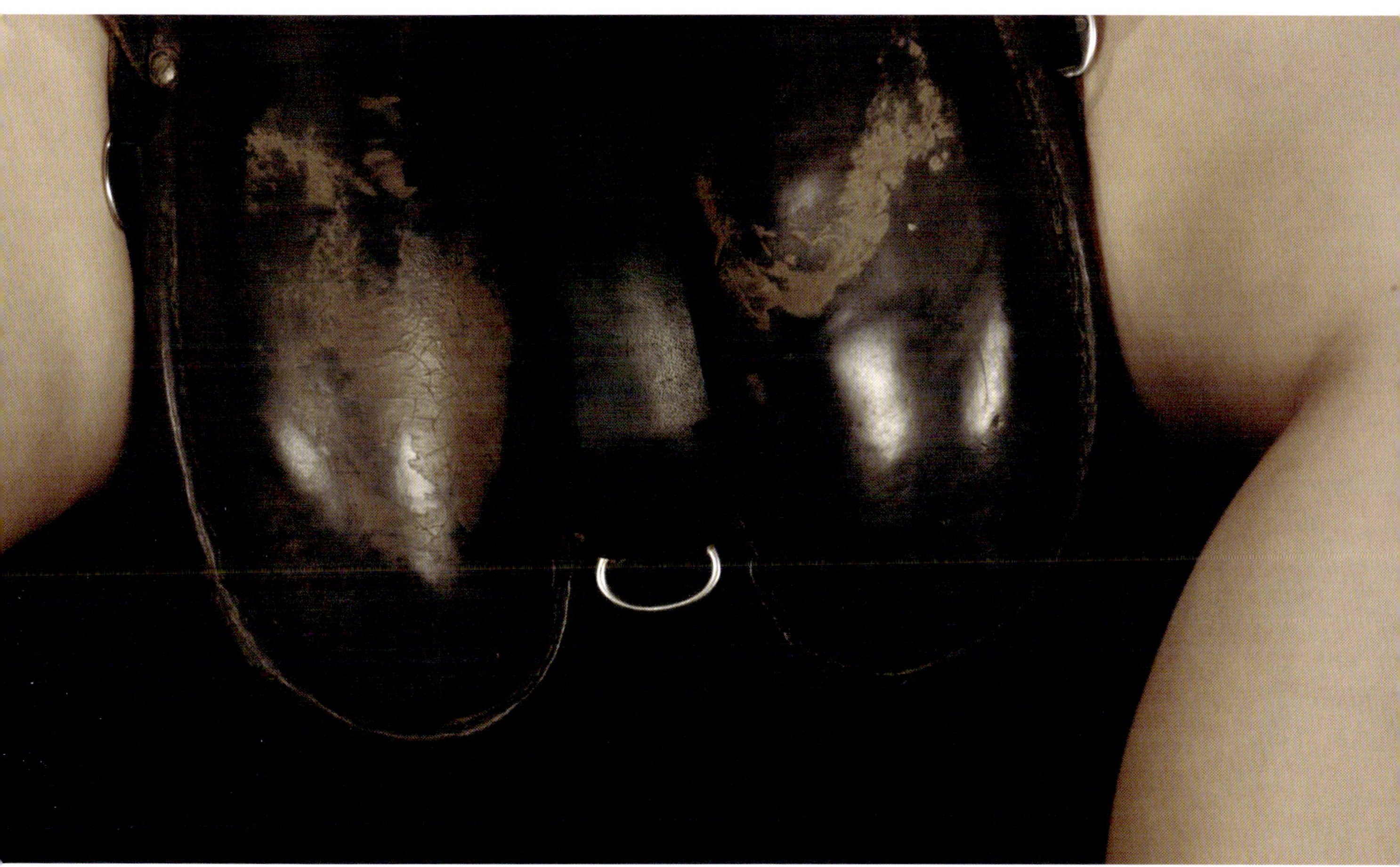

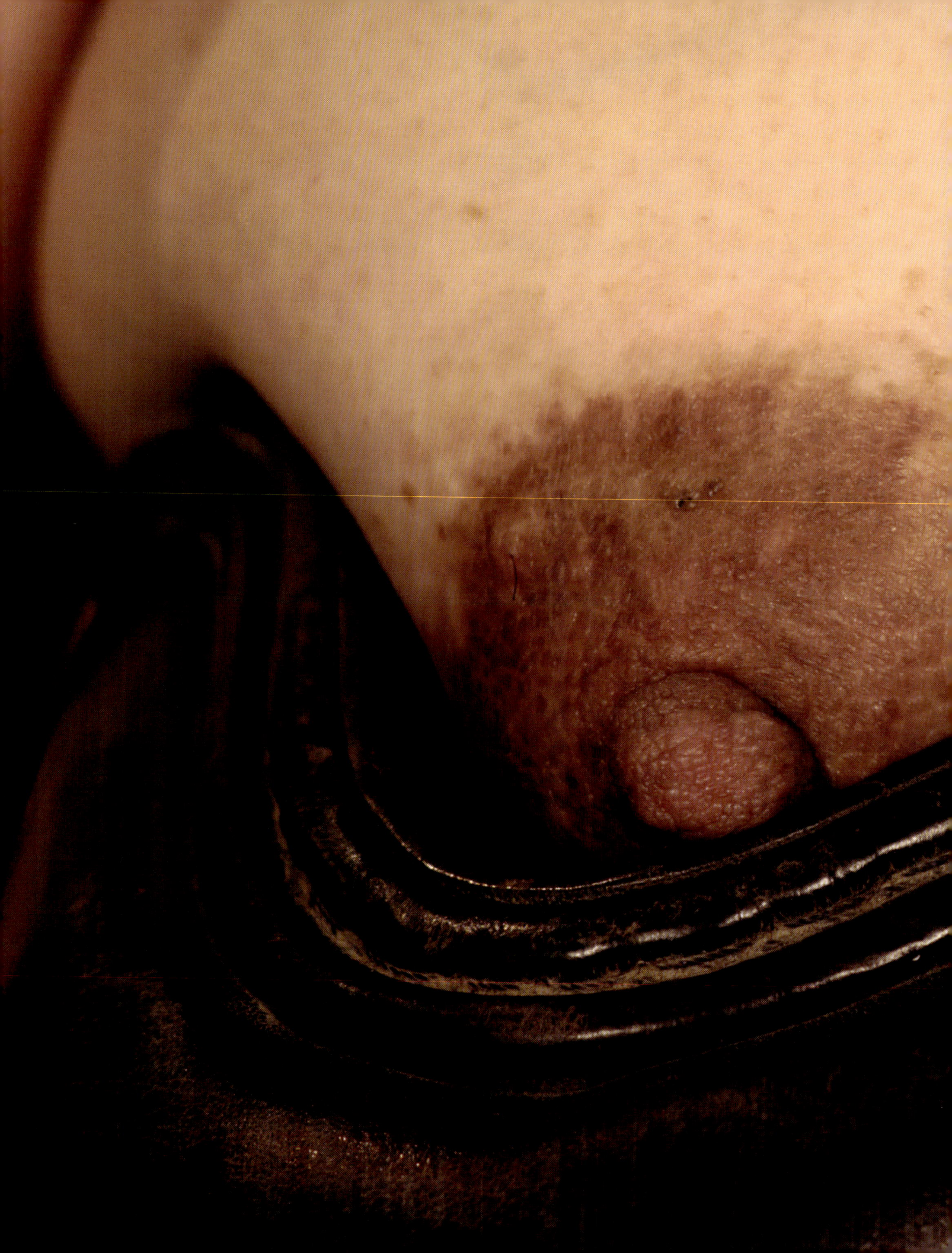

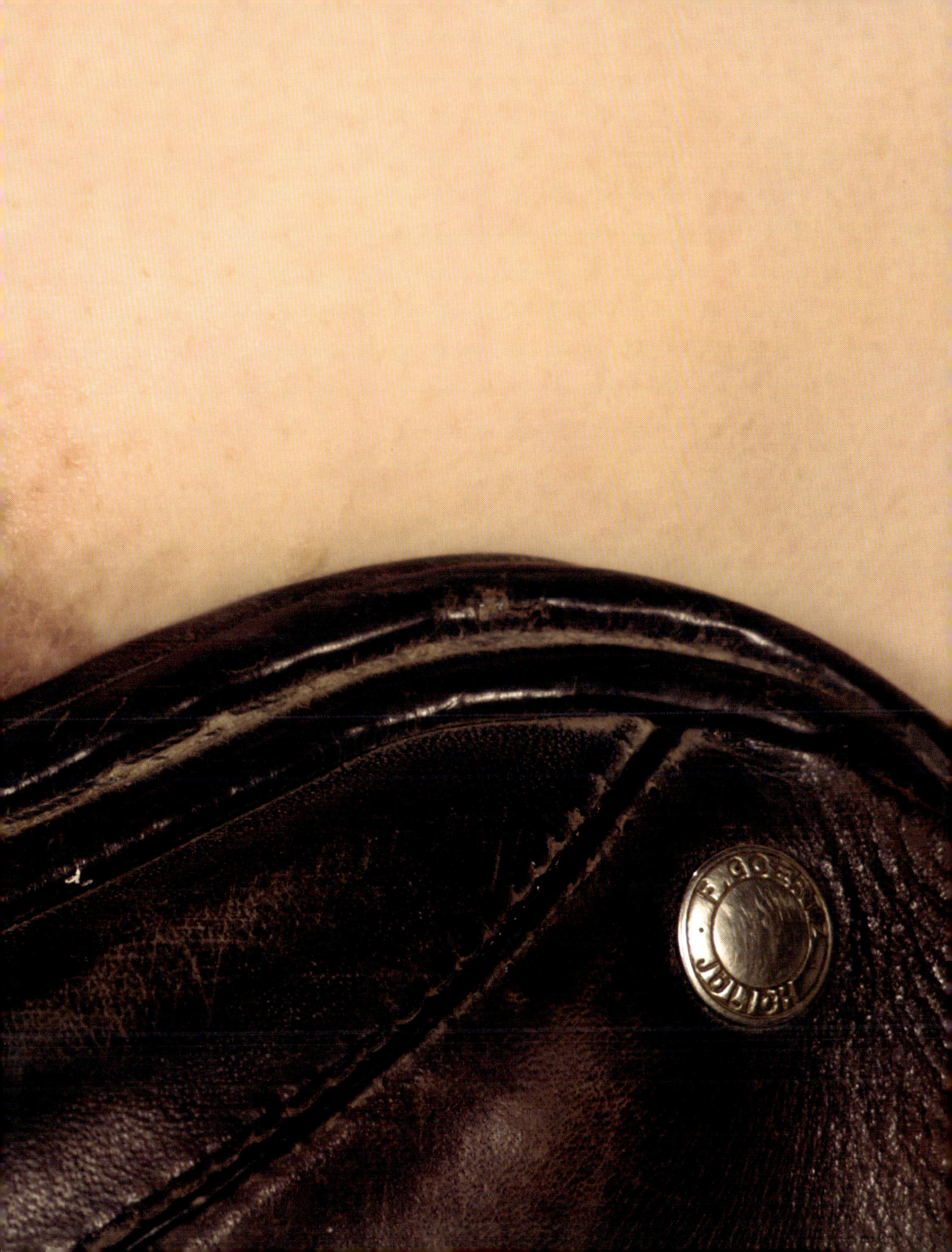
JULICH

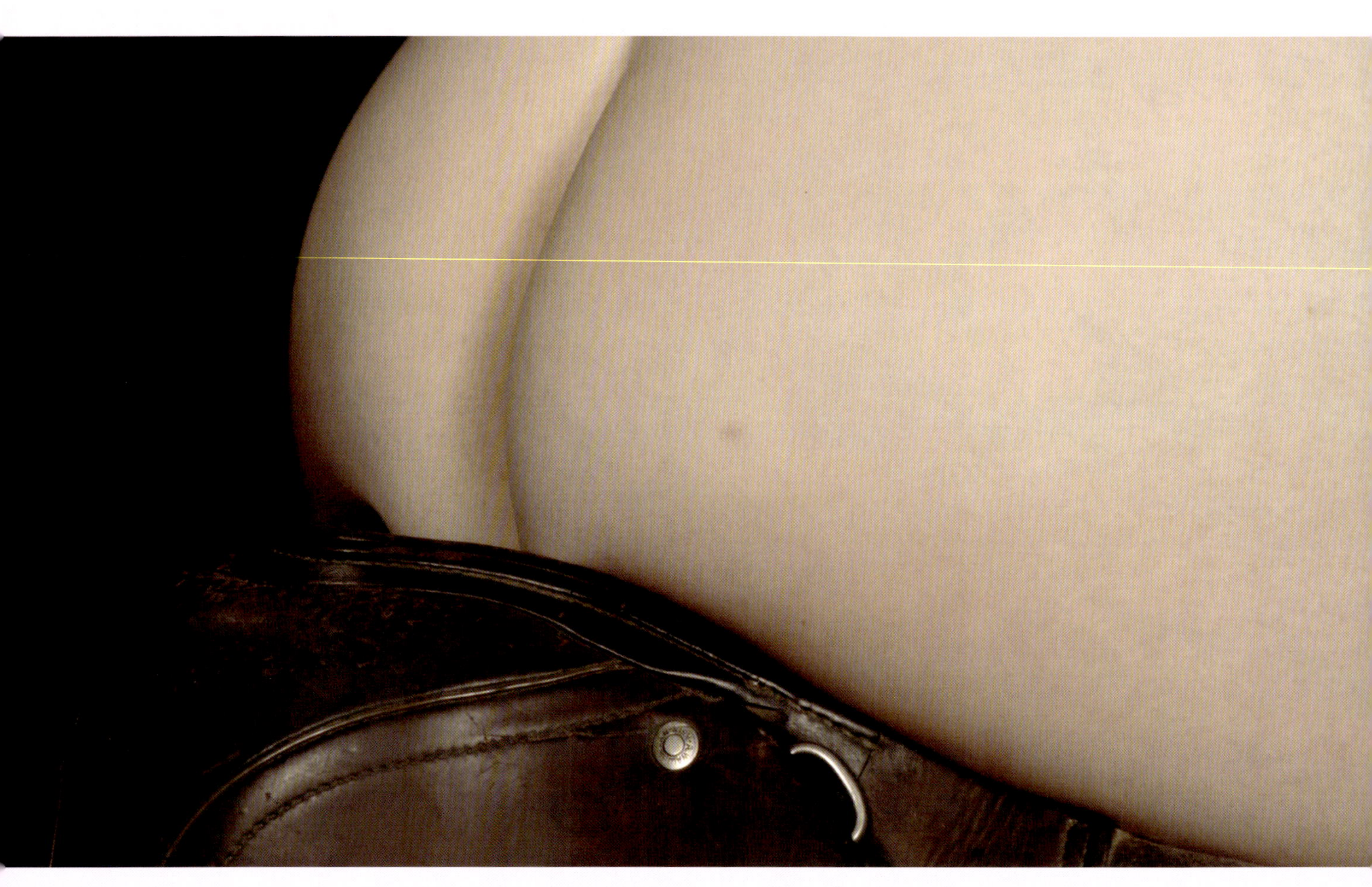

Pfauenloch

[Peacock Hole]
2018
color, sound
09:36 min

Plum Circus

2019
color, sound
12:00 min

Pomp

2020
color, silent
08:00 min

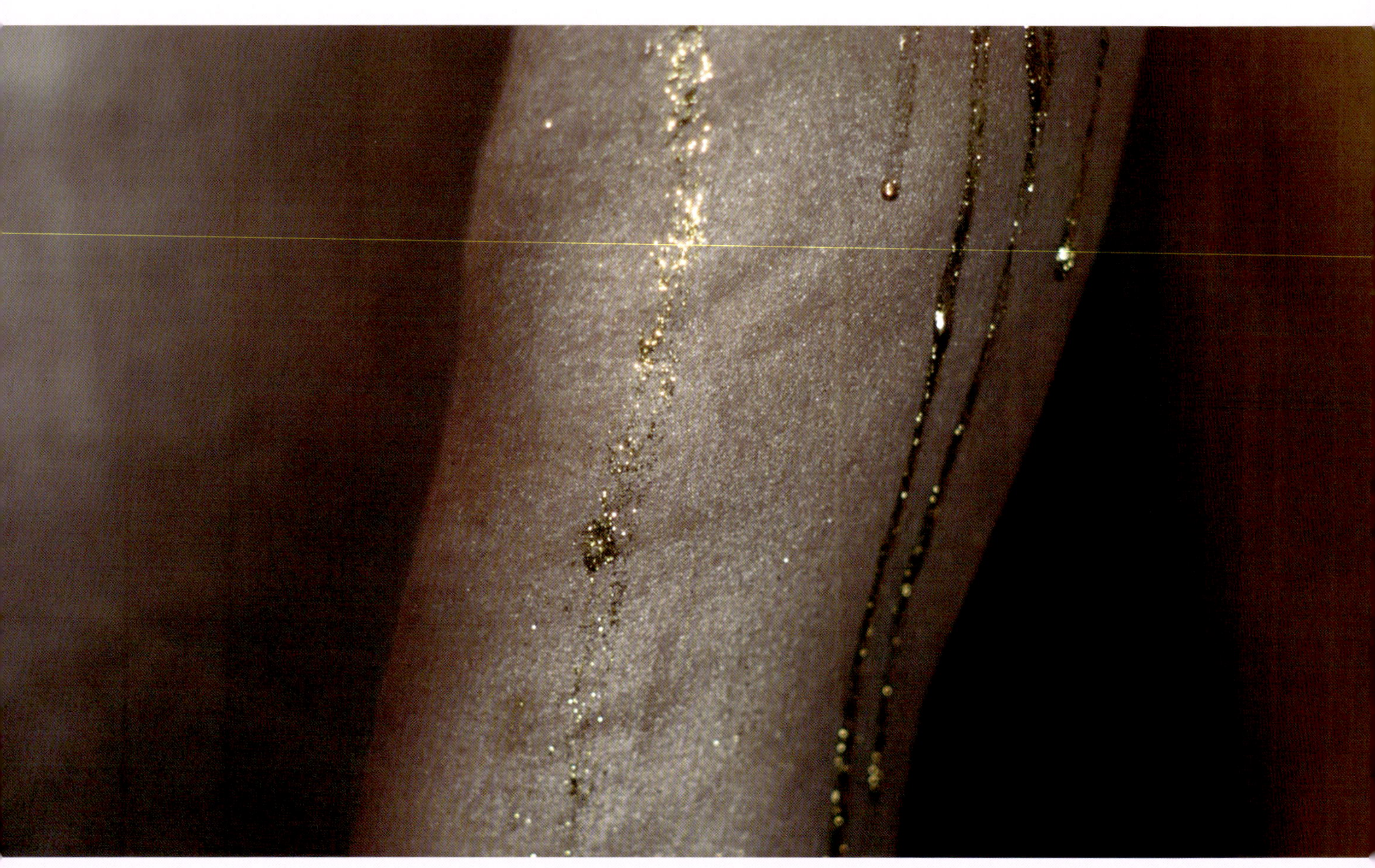

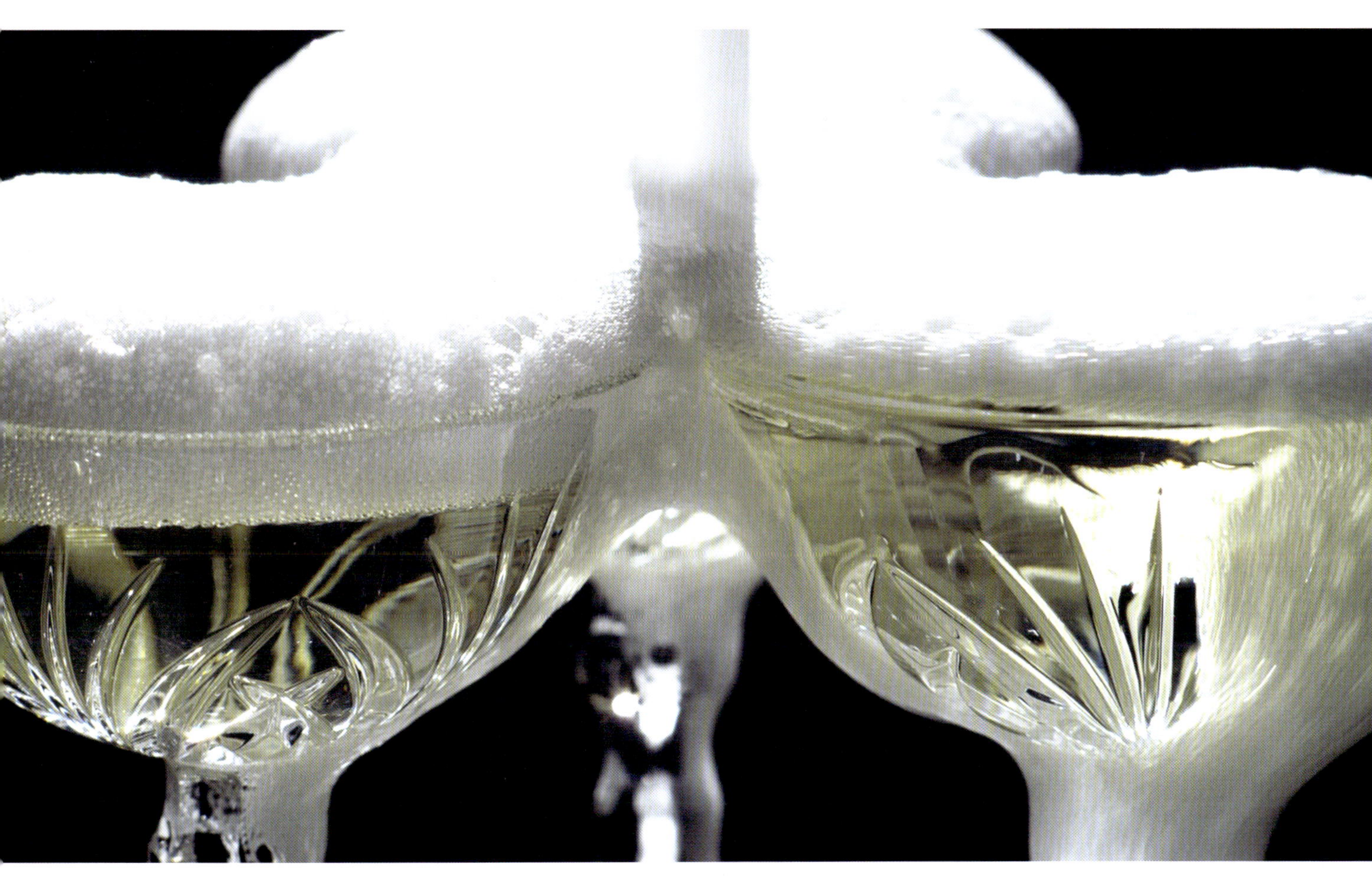

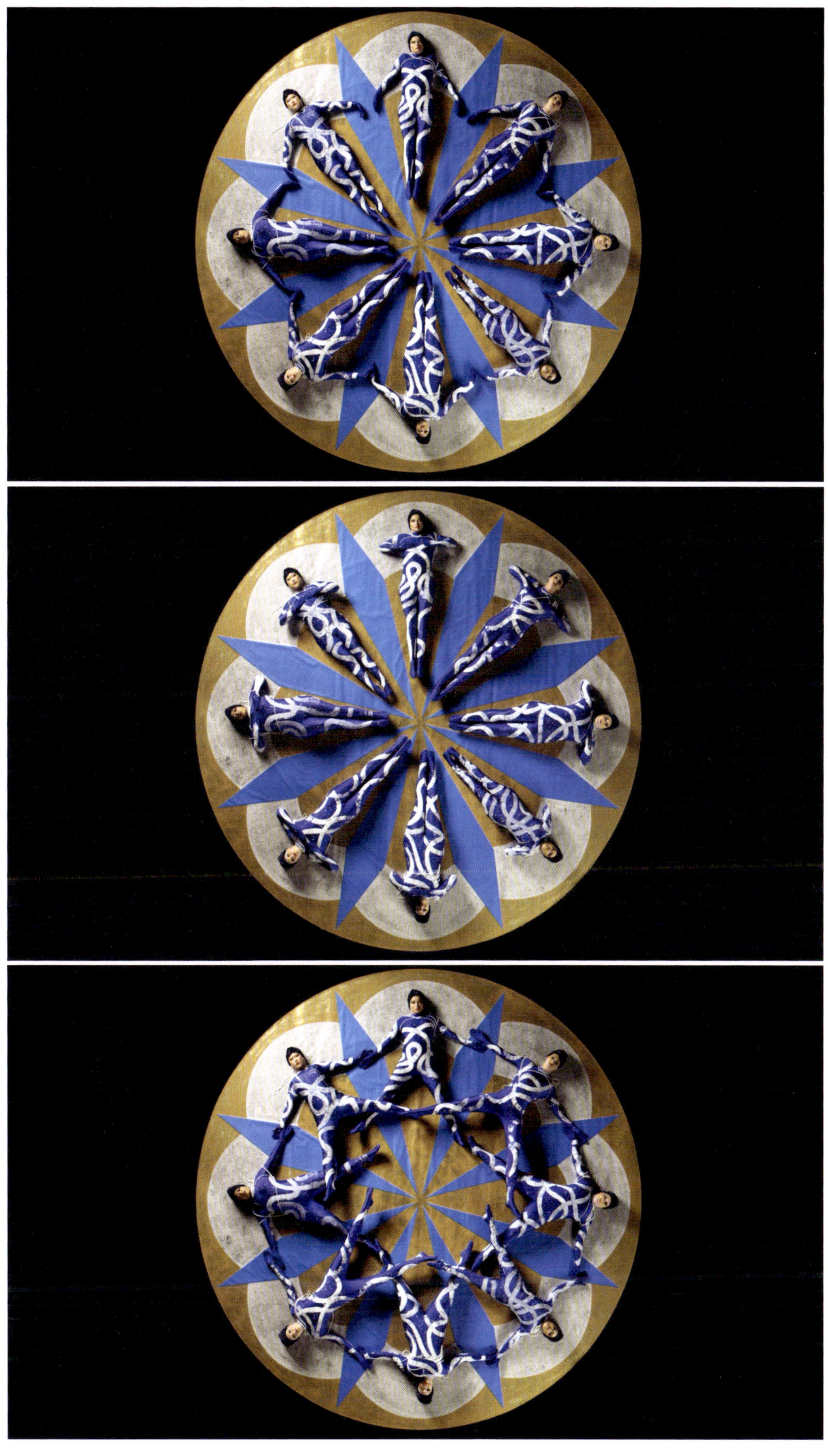

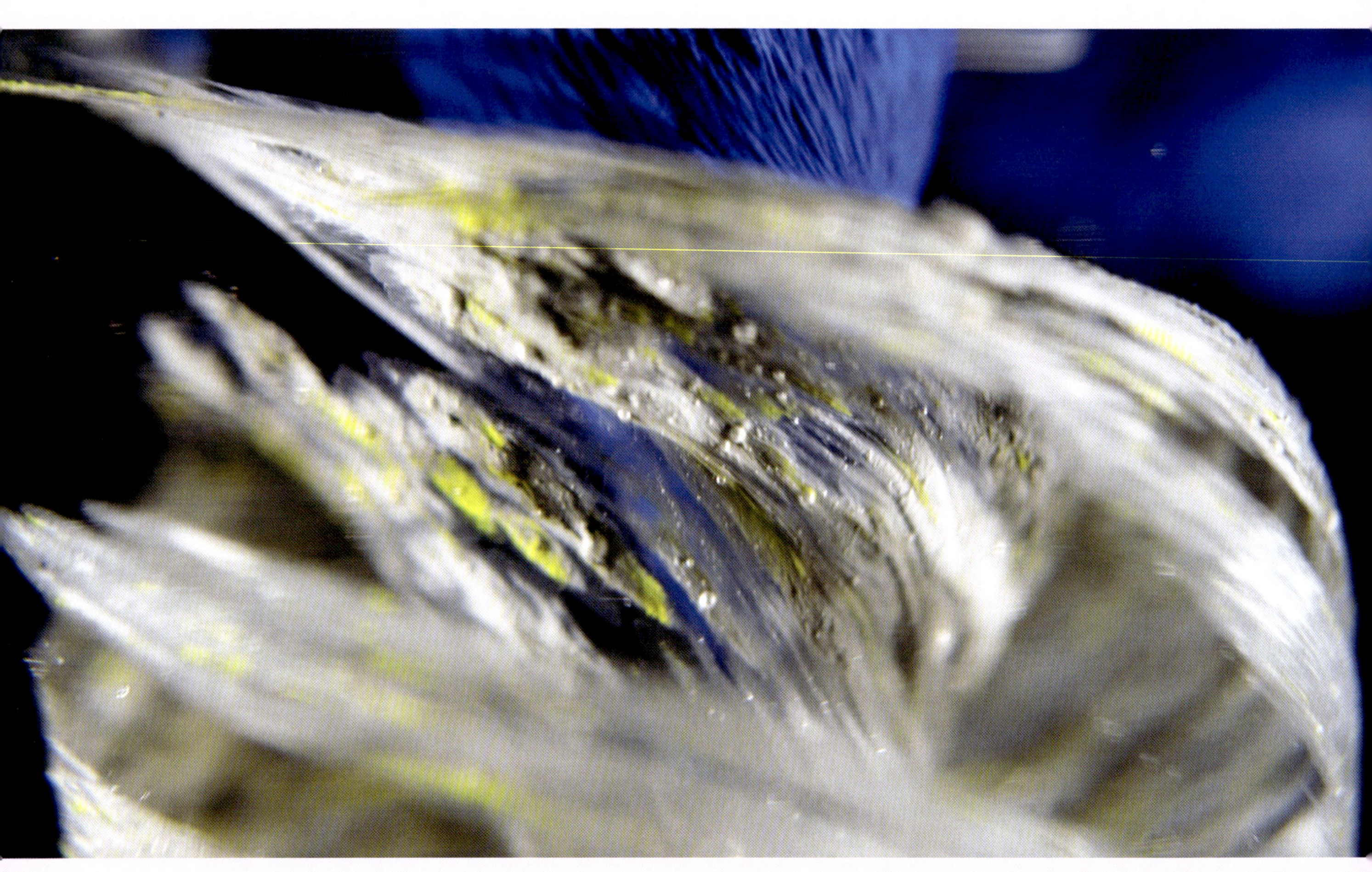

Golden Shadow

2022
color, sound, 2-channel
18:00 min

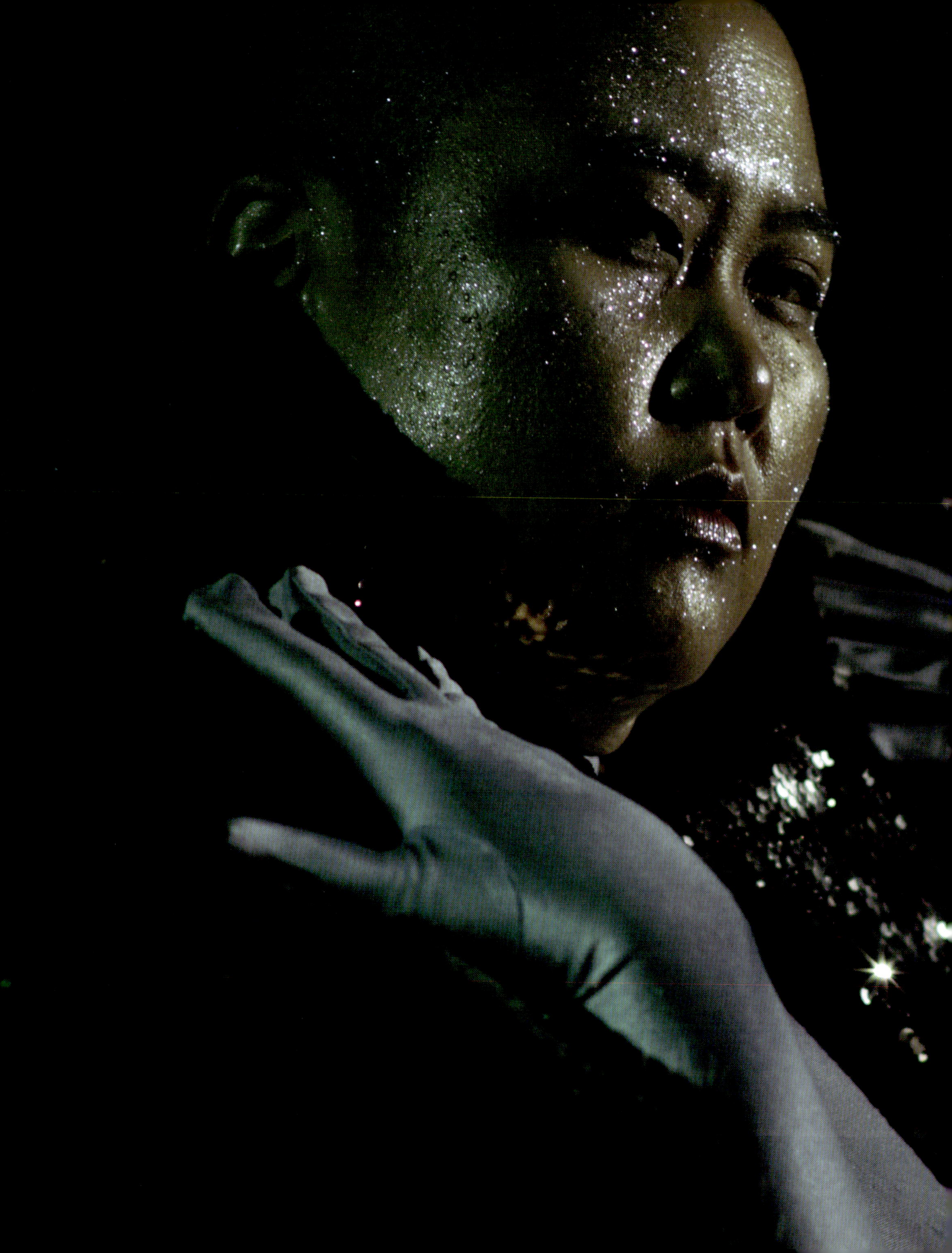

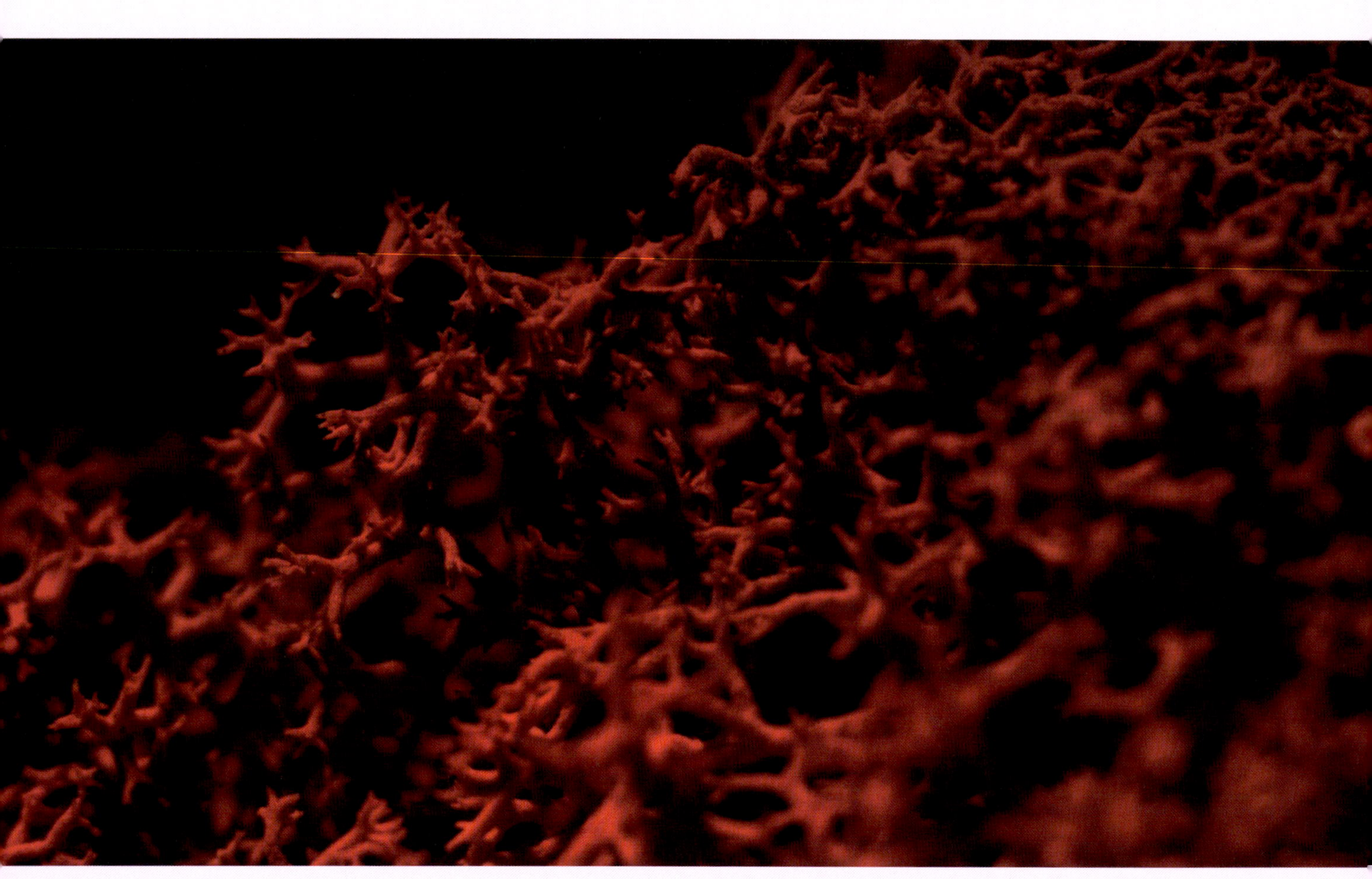

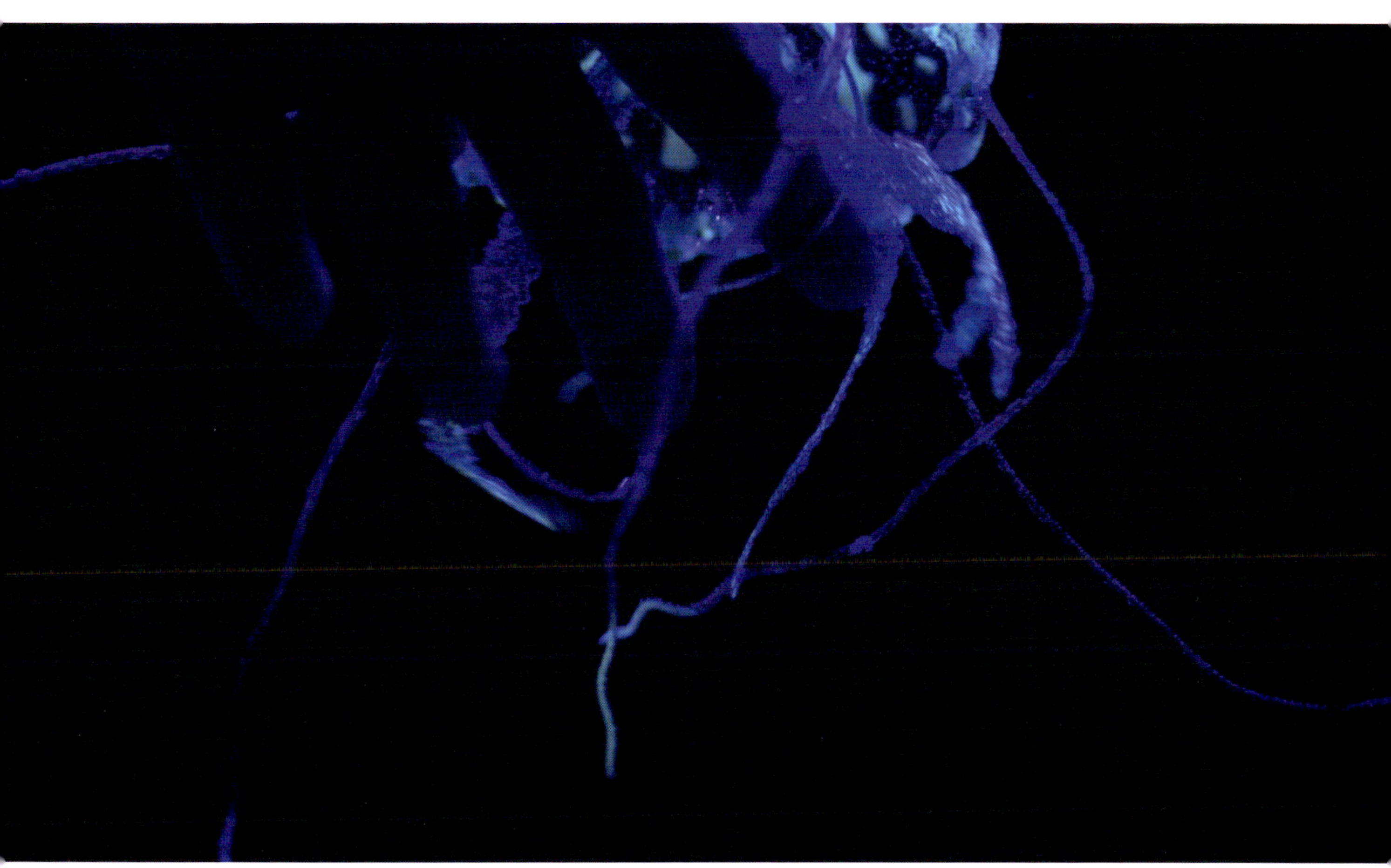

Making of

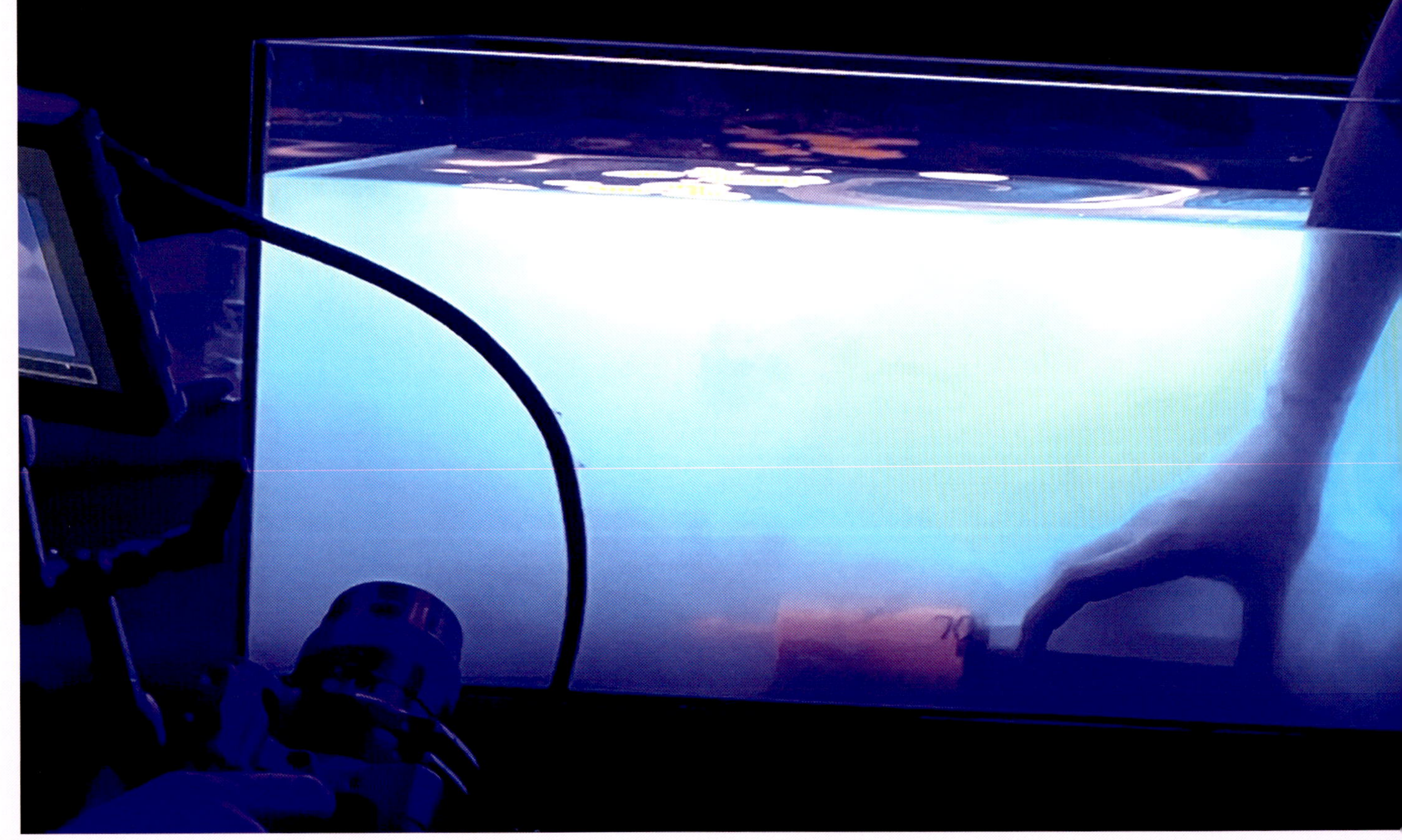

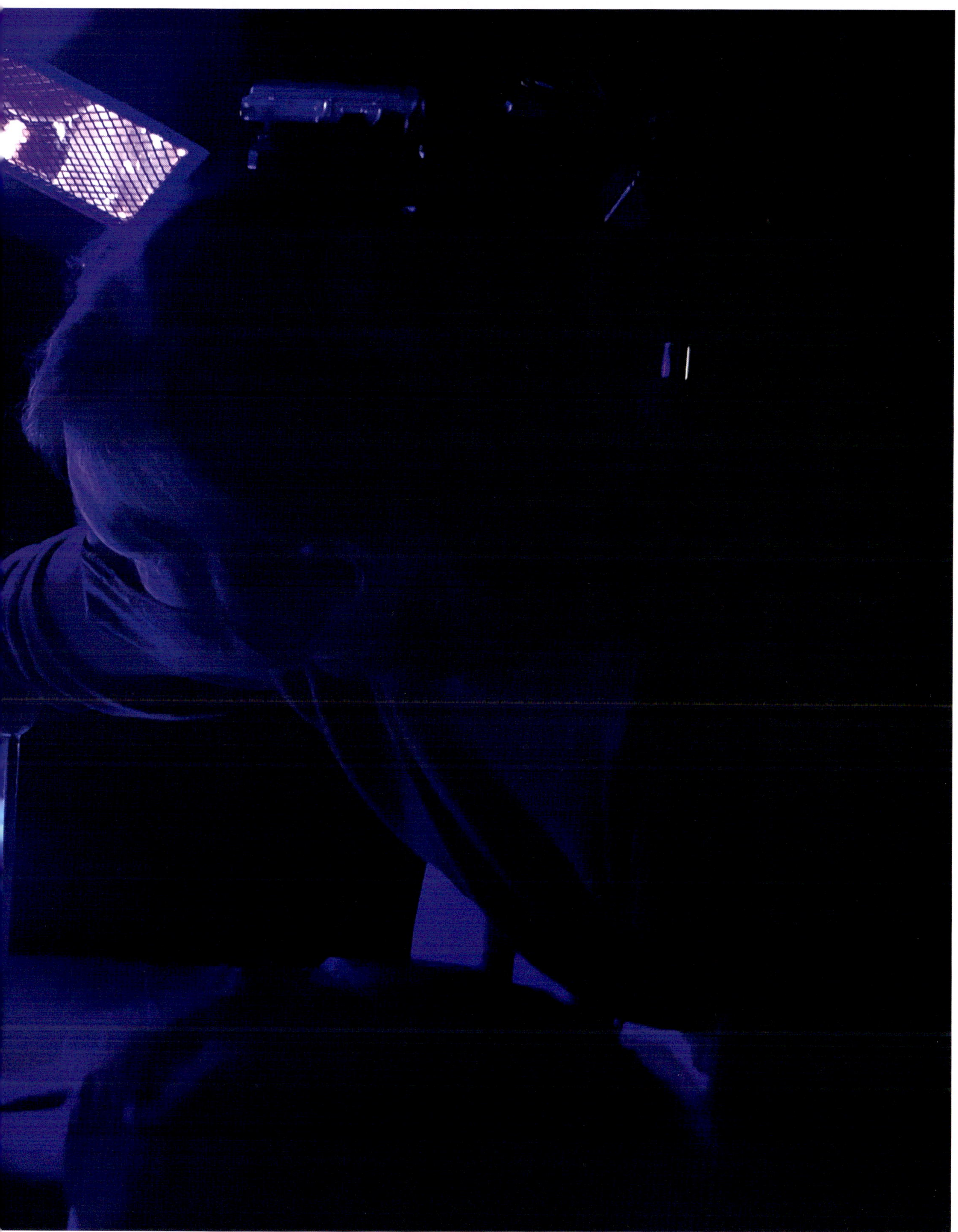

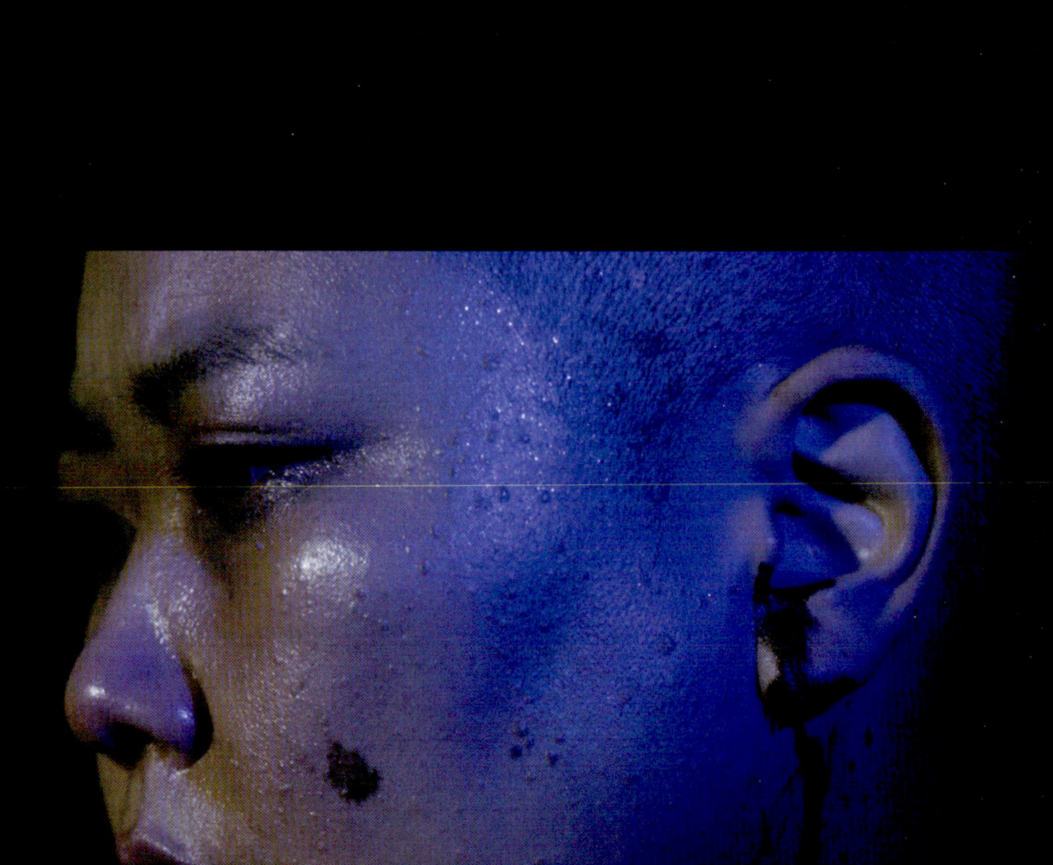

Hyo mit Rettungsdecke

Hyo – Close up
(Blut aus Ohr)
mit Rettungsdecke

Hyo – Close up
mit Rettungsdecke

Hyo am See
mit Kraken-Wesen
von hinten (Glitter auf ihr)

Hyo mit Krake
Close-up

Bonbon

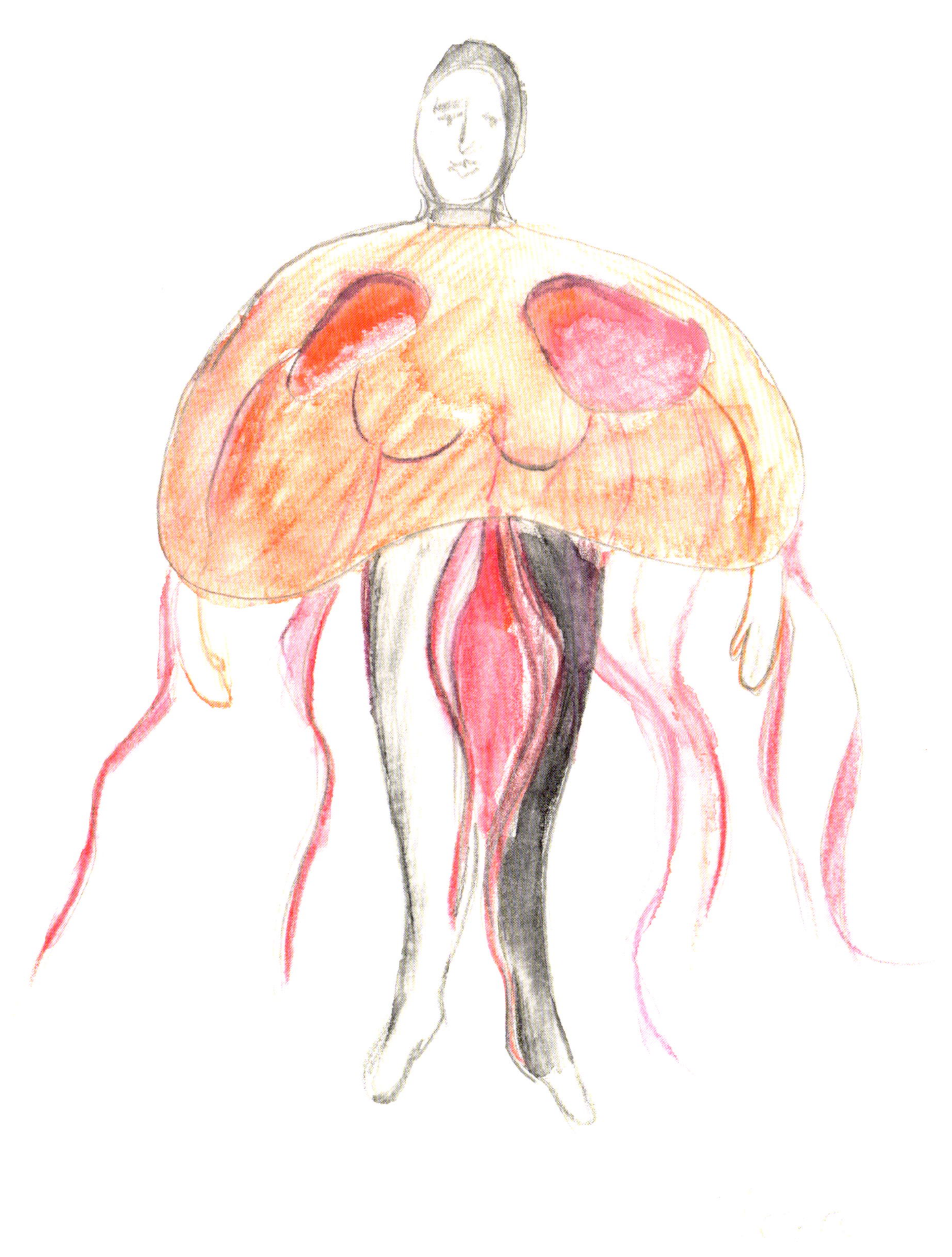

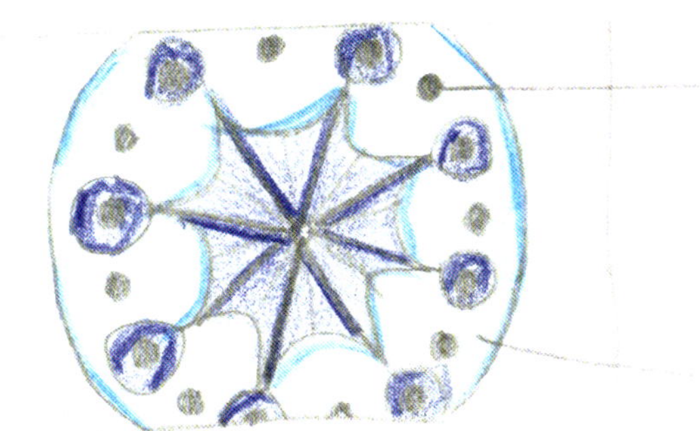

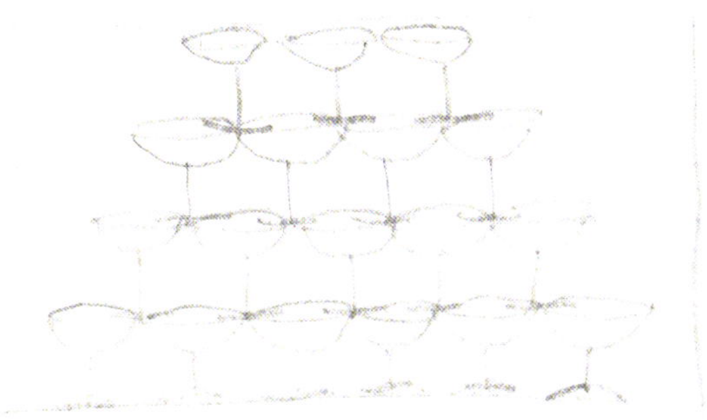

FINGERTANZ

DIVERSE
PAPERWEIGHT

Mimik: Stummfilmästhetik

3 Broccoli's tanzen
zu Musik (eher cool / Hiphop)
(oder doch sphärisch???)
keine Musik

Reigen um d. Dildo

2 Spargel tauchen
auf, gehen sehr
gerade + statisch in
Bildmitte -> schauen Broccoli
zu, sind erstaunt, schauen
in Kamera, schütteln Kopf
-> gehen hinter Broccoli
aus dem Bild

- Alle Perf. wieder
an Nabel / Kopf-schnüren
Äpfel an Schnüren (5x)
- Brunnen aus dem Nebel
kommt (Nebelmaschine ...)

- a + b reiben sich mit Liebe
ein (Latexhandschuhe)
hier auch close up

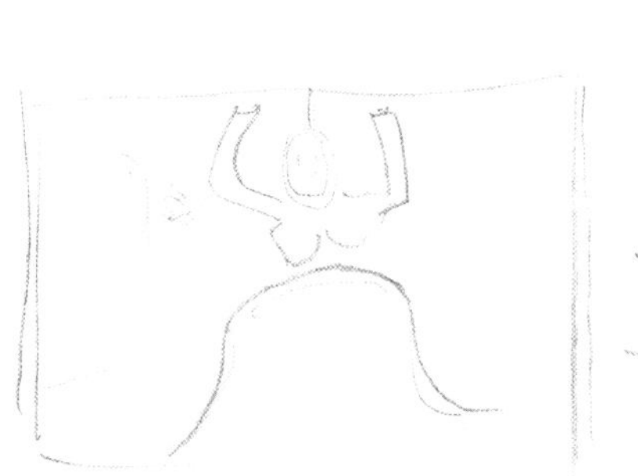

- d + e wollen Äpfel essen

- c schaut allen zu.
verdreht
die Augen eher abwesend /
elfenartig

Archive
of Senses

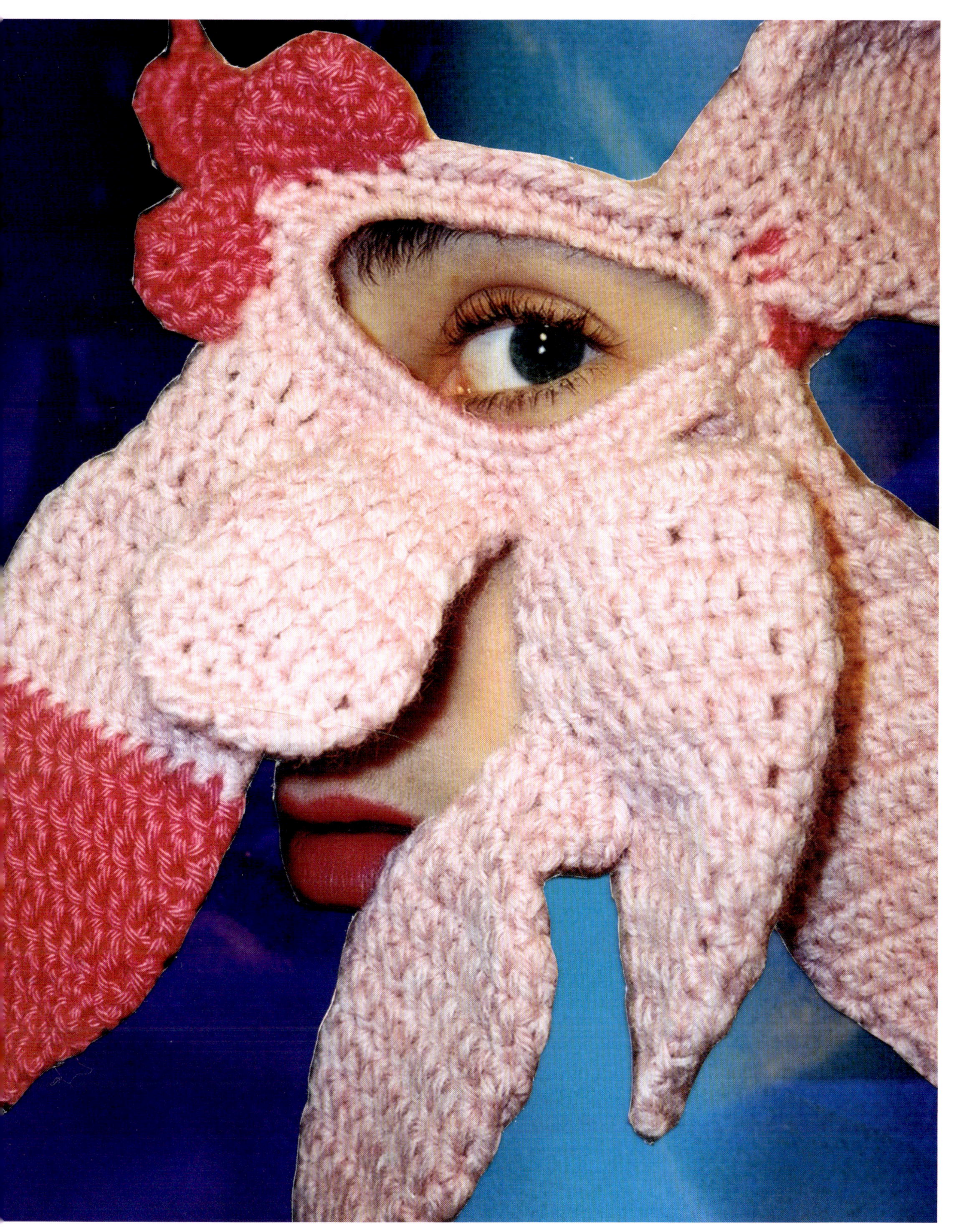

More Is More

Katrina Daschner in Conversation with Rike Frank

Rike Frank: *We first met in Vienna in the late 1990s and both spent some time in Mexico City in 1999–2000; the artist Uli Aigner had initiated a residency program at La Panaderia at that time. In 1999 you had your solo show "Ojos bien cerrados" there, and I curated "Never alone again" the following year, a group show including some of your collages. I'd like to start our conversation by asking what kind of time that was for you.*

Katrina Daschner: It was a very intense time ;-) My first association with Mexico is definitely my own coming-out, my first fulfilling love relationship with a woman. And an artistic time when I worked a lot, using relatively simple means. What else do I associate with it? The first experience of what a self-organized space can do. On one level La Panaderia was a gallery-like, very experimental art space, run by two artists, Yoshua Okon and Miguel Calderon. At the same time, there was this residency. Everything was organized in a totally low-key way. I was very impressed to see what a space like that is capable of creating and that this doesn't require a massive structure. This definitely led to me opening the Salon Lady Chutney in Vienna. So that was really a very good initial question, a lot of what still shapes me today started in Mexico.

R: You once talked about how after Mexico you increasingly got involved in political networks and also co-founded queer-feminist ones.

K: Yes, absolutely. When I opened Salon Lady Chutney with Johanna Kirsch and Stefanie Seibold in 2000, one reason was to have a performance space in the city, because at the time there was no such thing outside of theaters. The Tanzquartier and the brut didn't exist yet. So, in the years between the 60s–70s, when performance and actionism were very much present, and 2000 there was this big gap. We wanted to fill it. Another reason was that we were interested in the performative aspect in relation to gender.

At the same time, we thought of the space as a meeting place, which was clearly implied in the architecture of the space. It had an upstairs bar. I mean, all of this was actually tiny. But a network formed ... also for me personally, and it's still there today. Even though we never called the Salon a specifically queer-feminist space, it did turn out to be precisely that. Simply because we were running it, and because of who we invited and the program we put on. Pretty much simultaneously with this, I was part of the big organizing collective for the first Vienna Ladyfest. The friendships and alliances that resulted, including on a professional level, have lasted right up to the present day, for example with people I've worked with constantly in various contexts ever since, like Denice Bourbon, Sushi Mesquita, and Silk Graf. Interestingly, Amelia Groom asked me about the origins of my collective working practice. And it was only with that question that I realized this was connected to my own coming-out, that it was from then on that I became much more involved in feminist networks, working collectively. Definitely a lot more so than before. All the long-term collective projects started after 2000.

R: Your early collages are very outspoken and straightforward—they reject traditional role models and representations of feminine identity very explicitly and expand purely human bound bodies by means of crocheted masks and other applied and made up objects and costumes. Still, you remain clearly recognizable, often even appearing multiple times or as multiple you. Can you talk a bit about the transformation and multiplication of self and your working practice back then?

K: In these collages I was really trying to dissolve the idea of a stable subject. In the sense of the deconstruction of identity. So there's something you might call a collective, mutable "I", but not in a pathological way. A destabilized state as resistant force. Of course these were also self-portraits. I took them with an analogue pocket camera, a Yashica T5. I had this huge chaotic archive of 10 × 15cm prints, which I cut up with nail scissors and recombined in all kinds of ways, bringing out new non-existent places and relationships and other diverse layers. Most of them were shot in bathrooms, private and public ones. In retrospect I'd say they were definitely a safe space for me, somewhere everything was possible. A refuge, a space where outward action started to become possible. [...] With the crotchet masks I could keep certain parts shut off and expand them in other directions. In the sense of elongating the body. A lot of the collages from around this time at the end of the 90s also involve a sense of injury. Looking at these works now, at almost 50 years old, I would say this was also my personal way of dealing with certain experiences, that it was actually a form of visual #metoo activism, just different. But already back then I was consciously trying to make a transformation visible in the collages. It was really fun to make them: cutting up and striking back. I think a lot of them are quite funny, or let's say not exactly lacking humor.

R: Some of your early publications, such as the calendar "Do lesbians have better sex? Of course they do!" (2003) or the artist book Killing the Systems Softly *(2004) and later* Nouvelle Burlesque Brutal *(2012) were all published by Fotohof (Salzburg). I was wondering whether you ever saw yourself as a photographer?*

K: I don't think I've ever seen myself as a photographer in the traditional sense. Even though my main works were photographic for many years, my focus was on my performance in them, the performative act. So even at that point, directing was more important to me. I also didn't actually photograph a lot of the more narrative photographic series myself: I appeared in them and planned the staging and the image design, but someone else often actually took the pictures. Same thing with my films now. Of course as director I decide what images I want, but there's also the cinematographer bringing in a lot in this process. That's why I never really thought of myself as a photographer.

R: At the same time though it was —and it still is—crucial that your collages appeared in this context: namely, in the framework of an institution, which, founded in 1981, very early on shaped a discourse around photography in Austria and built relationships with international artists ... Although the history of performative self-representations in the medium of photography and the dismantling of stereotypical, primarily female role models was discussed and works by Cindy Sherman, among others, were exhibited, and although your works were in dialogue with these traditions, your practice clearly spoke from a different position. A practice that has clearly and intentionally opened up other places of desire.

K: I think an aspect that runs right through my work is that I've always been interested in taking the works to places where that kind of work doesn't quite fit. Coming from a different direction, commenting on another genre. The same in film nowadays—a lot of my works have been shown at film festivals over the last few years, and I'm interested in what happens there with a cinematic language heavily influenced by visual arts, sculpture, performance and theatrical languages. What happens with this in a film context, this displacement, I think this often shows up in my works. And if it starts feeling too smooth I notice a kind of restlessness forming inside me and I go looking for another space. I guess feeling truly at home isn't really my thing, it makes me suspicious.

R: Let's come back to the camera for a moment: At what point does the second person join in? When did you start handing the camera over to someone else? In early series like Jeanny *(1998) you were still using a delayed-action timer.*

K: It depended. I started doing this deliberately in film with *Hafenperlen*, in 2008. It was a conscious decision then and something I'd been thinking about for a long time. It wasn't really about handing the camera over. My consideration was that I'd worked in a very DIY mode until then and I felt a need to change that. To change the production process. I just felt quite strongly that queer content in the fine arts was often confined to a particular pigeonhole, kept small that way—like any feminist art, which is taken out for a certain period of time, only to be put neatly away again, mostly at the bottom of course. At that time I had the very strong feeling that I wanted to change the aesthetics of the works in such a way that I or we could inhabit a stronger position from which to speak. And also to reach people who might be quite far removed from feminist-queer contexts with a more easily engaging, more involving language. A language they can't turn away from so quickly because it somehow also draws them in emotionally ... and this way the effect can be stronger. In that sense it was definitely a political strategy, considering that, in the mainstream, a queer awareness like today didn't exist at that time. Lately I'm tending more towards wanting to simplify my practice again.

R: Maybe this is a good point to talk about materiality. Your collages, and also your films and your embroidery works are already all brought to life by combinations of materials. We've talked about networks and collective spaces you were involved with like Salon Lady Chutney and CLUB BURLESQUE BRUTAL. Your works function similarly, they also create encounters, haptic physicalities, differently interlaced textures ...

K: Yes, this has to do with the combination of materials, but also with the actions of embroidering, sewing, crochet as such. They're all craft techniques that carry within them the possibility of networking. Knitting is very different, there I have a pattern and I need a plan that I can follow. But with crochet, embroidery, and sewing I can start somewhere and from there it develops in all directions. It's much freer, in that sense. Similar to corral life forms; something that runs throughout the films thematically. They also have no linear narrative. And this is also possible with techniques like crochet and embroidery. You just start somewhere and it expands from there.

R: To what extent have you already worked out the motif when you start the crochet—like the masks in the 1990s, or the embroidery in more recent works?

K: Yeah, this is exactly what I was trying to get at—it's not worked out in advance, which is why I usually keep working with small-format materials. Because I really appreciate how I can start anywhere with these techniques. So just like with a drawing or a sketch I just start with no prior plan. That's how those masks were made in the 90s, where in retrospect you could think they do all have some things in common, there must have been some sort of plan. But there wasn't. The embroideries too, which accompany my films as something like embroidered storyboards, again there are only very vague initial ideas, I think about the films but there's no preliminary sketch or anything. Even though I call them "Embroidered Storyboards," they're really mental, conceptual storyboards that arise in parallel. Not like my actual drawn storyboards, which really do serve as support for the actual film shoot.

R: I didn't realize that.

K: It could also be a meditative space where I can draft things, get things straight in my head. I don't know ... other people might go for a run or something to bring structure to certain processes.

R: Is there a back-and-forth exchange for you between developing a storyboard and the "Embroidered Storyboards"? When you say something gets clarified, does that include artistic decisions?

K: Yes, definitely. Artistic decisions become clear in the process. Embroidery is an activity or artistic technique where I do start somewhere and get to somewhere, and this is visible. And the thoughts unfold in parallel, I mean you're really concentrated while doing it and can also gain clarity about something else at the same time.

R: Embroidery in free space is something that makes me look at the works really differently now.

K: Yes, when I'm embroidering it's absolutely a flow. And I totally see how you

“Although I’ve never worked with sculpture in the traditional sense, it wasn’t by chance that I studied sculpture, because physically tangible visual art always interested me most, and that’s still true.”

could get the idea that these things were planned. Especially on the black linen cloth. But linen is a fabric with a quantifiable thread count, which makes it easy to stitch straight lines. The cloth pre-sets it, so to speak. Embroidery on non-countable cloth looks totally different, tending towards the organic or amorphic. But in terms of the flow or the process it gets worked out of the material.

R: Your description of the interaction with the material and how this plays into artistic decision-making and form-finding processes immediately brings me to the films. Because here the manifold impact of the materials is even more evident. They are visibly—and palpably—part of the plot, the direction, and of the cinematic language. Their materiality—texture and form, their use and application—clearly also steers and co-directs the narrative. I’d like to talk about the research processes that precede your choice of materials.

K: I like how we’re moving from the materials to the films because this really is how the process often starts. I collect materials, from marbles to sequins and hair, and this also defines the color of the film. The films have a color atmosphere from the very start. It’s one of the threads a film is developed from. Along with vague mental images of staging and places, choreographies, and people.

R: The location has special meaning in the film series Hiding in the Lights. *In reference to Arthur Schnitzler’s* Traumnovelle *[Dream Story], you very specifically chose a site for each of the eight chapters. They are all linked to the theater and were determined very early in the development of the project.*

K: Yes, but the very first thing, the skeleton, so to speak, of this eight-part-series, was probably the thought that every film has a very specific structure of desire. And I had this subdivided from the very start, when nothing else was defined ... self-love or collectivity or also the paradisic versus the horror, the attraction of the uncanny ... starting from that I started looking for these places, like you say, theatrical settings, theatrical audience architecture, that seemed to fit these specific aspects of sexuality and desire. The heart of *Traumnovelle* is the masked ball. Today that would probably be a sex party. And in the different areas different things happen, providing for all interests. And I divided these spaces that open up in the novel into separate short films.

R: This brings us to a point I find extremely exciting, the way you describe it: the interdependence between structures of desire, places, and the materiality of things, textures, and props, of costumes, light, and atmospheres. All of these embody the tactility and haptics that you are interested in, and so does the interplay between human and non-human elements in the stories.

K: My thinking is basically visual and tactile. I can’t create this in a story-based narrative. That would be doing something completely different. Although I’ve never worked with sculpture in the traditional sense, it wasn’t by chance that I studied sculpture, because physically tangible visual art always interested me most, and that’s still true. Also in film, what matters to me is to create something that can be experienced with the body and the eyes in a tactile way. And this is done, besides the work with architecture, makeup, or props, very much through editing. Maybe that takes us back to the question of collage technique. All the way through, nothing is or remains purely a backdrop. How costumes, architecture, or landscape but also the performers are filmed, through image composition and then editing: the symbioses that happen have no hierarchies. Or at least that’s the goal, that there should be one filmic body which, as you said before, merges the human and non-human, the conjoint protagonist or body of the film.

R: In an earlier conversation you mentioned that you were 15 years old when you took part in a stage design workshop at the Thalia Theater in Hamburg; you were taught old-style stage set design techniques like marbling ... and before you came to study in Vienna you started a tailoring apprenticeship at the Staatsoper in Berlin. Theater, tailoring, and transformation of materials in narrative are already present there. You just said that you think visually. You keep emphasizing the eye. At the same time, it’s a visuality that’s not centered on the eye as such. Instead it decentralizes the gaze and viewer's position, it takes me out of the purely optical, a dominance of the optical and distanced optical relationship that is, after all, often a controlled one. Just as the exhibition transposes me, the visitor, into a body-(exhibition-)space relation, deliberately breaking from traditional White Cube regimes.

K: Yes, I agree with this. Seeing as visual process is mainly a means to an end. Like flushing everything *into* the body. It's definitely about a whole-body experience. That's how the exhibition at the Kunsthalle is laid out.

R: And this space implies particular options and strategies for action.

K: I'm not sure it comes with strategies but it definitely comes with options. And I think the exhibition gives visitors a lot of freedom to make decisions: how they want to stand in relation to the images, how close, how far away. What they want to see. And starting on the films is also possible at any point because the films don't follow a linear narration.

R: Yes, that's how I experienced it.

K: Because of the varying lengths of the films, new visual combinations emerge between the films over and over again. Between *Perlenmeere* and *Golden Shadow* for instance, or also when looking at *Pferdebusen*. Basically they comment on each other and enter into various kinds of collaborations. And the decision to work with a black carpet for the exhibition on one hand and on the other with silver mirrored dancefloors that grow like lake scenery or tongues out of the films—whilst also acting as mini-stages, which visitors are invited to step on ... this leads to a switching between onstage and offstage situations.

These questions—Where does the stage start? Where does it end? Who is part of a performance?—they run through many of my works, and I was able to develop these aspects specifically for this spatial setting together with the curator, Övül Ö. Durmuşoğlu. Another thought was to keep the main display mostly black and silver so that color enters the room through the films and the clothing of the visitors. In the mirroring of the moving image and the people moving in the space, the color and the activity in the room also change continuously. The curtains are also part of that.

R: I spoke earlier about the strategies of action because it's also a matter of what stories get written. You often say this is all a political struggle, too. Maybe this is too dense a way to put it, but the structural, political work you've been doing for decades and your artistic work are not easy to separate. And in that sense all the materials, all the protagonists in the films pursue an agenda that goes beyond the narrative. All the elements present in the films, in the exhibitions are part of this enduring work, of constantly making space for very specific structures of desire, that is, for very particular forms of knowing, of co-existing to which forms of life, cosmologies, and worldviews are linked.

K: I'm glad you mention this because it relates on a different level to what we briefly talked about earlier in terms of textiles and networks. The things you mentioned, the lesbian, queer, feminist networks, the collaborations or forms of co-existence, they shape my life to a huge extent. It's especially important for my films, where I've worked with almost the same cast and almost the same production team every time for many years. The films do not emerge collectively but they're still collaborations. And without the individual protagonists and what they stand for artistically and politically and who they very concretely are, the films would never have been what they are. Most of the performers are artists themselves, queer artists, who also bring aspects of their real lives into the film. Even if it's far removed from a documentary film, there are documentary elements present, not automatically on an obvious level, but of course the films are talking about or documenting some kind of queer life. And to come back to the change in production methods, that decision was also about propagating something that might not really be there yet, just to assert it in an art context, to create space for it, to make it visible, thinkable and also not to start at the bottom but posit it in the sense of a utopia. And over

"Sometimes it's only sentences that inspire me. With Nabokov and Schnitzler's *Traumnovelle* I also felt resentment and anger, which made me want to rewrite something, to fill in stories that weren't being told and still aren't often told, to add the feminist and queer stories."

many years we've managed to envision some things this way that actually have become real by now.

R: How did you end up deciding to study art? Did you start out thinking that art would be the medium for imagining utopias and making assertions as you called it just now?

K: As you mentioned earlier, I initially wanted to become a costume designer and I saw most potential for this in the theater. But art was also something I looked at on my own from early on, I still remember the Boltanski exhibition vividly, I was probably around 14 then and my art teacher at school had told me about it. Also Jan Hoet's documenta IX. Later, when I was in Hamburg in 1995 I saw Cindy Sherman at the Deichtorhallen and on the same day the *Heidi* cycle by Mike Kelley and Paul McCarthy at the Kunstverein. I still remember all this like it was today. A really formative experience, almost physical. From that day on I wanted to be an artist, no question about it. Those shows brought together so many things I'm still interested in today.

R: Before we come to an end, I'd like to talk about the role of literature and literary characters, because both—already in the collages—have a huge influence on your work and we have not yet addressed this aspect at all.

K: That's right. In the collages, characters from literary texts, novels and songs become my companions, so to speak. Then there are fictional characters, you could say "sisters in crime." I've subtitled many photographic works pretending they were film stills, kind of turning them into films that never existed. Also, texts often provided templates for large-scale exhibitions. Starting with my piece *Dolores* (2005), which is based on Nabokov's *Lolita.* I told it from her perspective, which changes the whole story of course. It became a room installation at the Kunsthalle Krems, then later in adapted forms at the Kunsthalle Wien, Prague and Brest. *Täterin* is based on the play with almost the same title by Thomas Jonigk, *Täter.* I take bits of the literature in a fragmentary, atmospheric way. Sometimes it's only sentences that inspire me. With Nabokov and Schnitzler's *Traumnovelle* I also felt resentment and anger, which made me want to rewrite something, to fill in stories that weren't being told and still aren't often told, to add the queer and feminist stories. To correct or complete something. If I worked with a literary template it was mostly the language itself that interested me. There has always been a sensual element to language and visual language. Especially with Schnitzler, he opened a lot of visual spaces inside my thoughts. Otherwise I wouldn't pay so much attention to it.

R: I was wondering to what extent your experience of showing films in the context of film festivals differs from an exhibition context? Do the works get a different reception? Do the conversations differ in the issues and discourses they address?

K: I can definitely say that it makes a huge difference to me whether I show my works in a film context or in exhibitions. The shared experience of the movie theater as distinct from moving alone through an exhibition space, where I make many decisions myself, both have their advantages and disadvantages, or to put it better, I wouldn't want to miss either. In short film programs there's mostly a lot of interest in mutual exchange between the film makers. It might have something to do with how in the Q&As you get to hear other film makers express their positions directly, which makes a huge difference in terms of the exchange. At Oberhausen these discussions cover a lot and the questions vary widely.

R: And how are these things different in relation to your films?

K: In a film context we talk much more about surfaces, textures, my interest in haptics and tactile elements, the film as perceptible *Gesamtkörper*. Sometimes I actually miss that in the art world. There I sometimes get the feeling that it's about the most obvious thing, i.e. that these are queer films. Of course they are. And that's important to me. But it's also about so much more. About aesthetic questions, about places, and about all the things we've been talking about. And I think in an art context all this almost gets pushed into the background while questions of identity and identity politics are magnified.

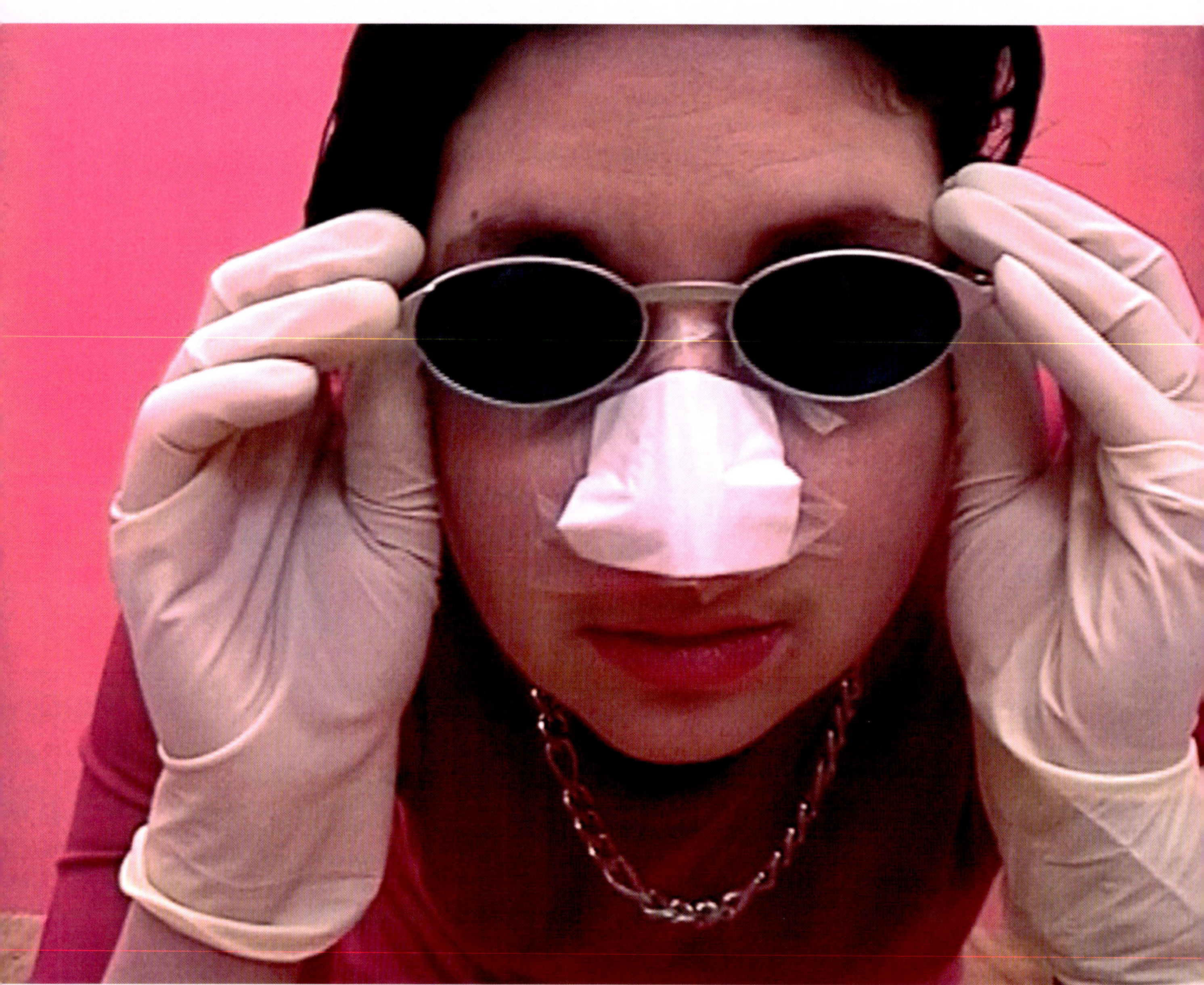

INTESTINO
GRUESO

Works Presented

Lesbian Teletentakel #1, 2022
Lesbian Teletentakel #2, 2022
Lesbian Teletentakel #3, 2022
Lesbian Teletentakel #4, 2022
Lesbian Teletentakel #5, 2022
Lesbian Teletentakel #6, 2022

All 140 cm x 200 cm
Embroidery on sewn fabric, artificial hair, brass, yarn
Courtesy the artist / Georg Kargl Fine Arts
Lesbian Teletentakel #2, 2022: Collection: Artothek des Bundes

Sister Siren (Silver-Gray), 2022
approx. 100 cm x 260 cm (d: 35 cm)
Concrete, brass, artificial hair, brass chain, neon string
Courtesy the artist / Georg Kargl Fine Arts

Sister Siren (White), 2022
approx. 100 cm x 260 cm (d: 35 cm)
Concrete, brass, acrylic glass tube, artificial hair, brass chain, neon string
Courtesy the artist / Georg Kargl Fine Arts

Sister Siren (Lilac), 2022
approx. 100 cm x 260 cm (d: 35cm)
Concrete, brass, acrylic glass tube, artificial hair, brass chain, neon string
Courtesy the artist / Georg Kargl Fine Arts

Sister Siren (Blue), 2022
approx. 100 cm x 260 cm (d: 35cm)
Concrete, brass, acrylic glass tube, artificial hair, brass chain, neon string
Courtesy the artist / Georg Kargl Fine Arts

Sister Siren (Red), 2022
approx. 100 cm x 260 cm (d: 35 cm)
Concrete, brass, acrylic glass tube, artificial hair, brass chain, neon string
Courtesy the artist / Georg Kargl Fine Arts

Embroidered Storyboards

Glühende Qualle (Glowing Jelly), 2021
44,5 cm x 44,5 cm framed
Threads on fabric
Collection: mumok—Museum moderner Kunst Stiftung Ludwig Wien

Grüner Faltenwurf (Green Drapery), 2018
44,5 cm x 44,5 cm framed
Threads on fabric
Courtesy the artist

Panele (Panels), 2015
44,5 cm x 44,5 cm framed
Threads on fabric
Courtesy the artist

Las Vegas, 2015
44,5 cm x 44,5 cm framed
Threads on fabric
Courtesy the artist

Water Beings on Neon Fabric

Burning Coral, 2021
23,5 cm x 23,5 cm framed
Threads on fabric
Courtesy the artist

Neon Medusa, 2021
23,5 cm x 23,5 cm framed
Threads on fabric
Courtesy the artist

Basic Stage (Collective Energy), 2022
Dimensions: Variable
Black dance floor, flitter machine, flitter
Courtesy the artist / Georg Kargl Fine Arts

Films

Parole Rosette, 2012
09:00 min
4K Video, color, silent
Courtesy the artist / sixpackfilm

<u>Director, script:</u> Katrina Daschner
<u>Starring:</u> Frankie Fierce, Cunt, Denise Kottlett, Don Chanel, Dorisa, Ehfer, Ernesta Imperialista, Hyo, Miss Bourbon, Oh Wildnis, Shu La Shu, Subsilk
<u>Cinematography:</u> Hannes Böck
<u>Editing:</u> Hannes Böck, Katrina Daschner
<u>Choreography:</u> Stefanie Sourial
<u>Lighting:</u> Johannes Gruber, Hannes Böck
<u>Costumes:</u> Andreas Riegler, Markus Pires-Mata
<u>Make-up:</u> Diego Rojas O., Kali Edri, Penelope Uttenthaler
<u>Direction assistant:</u> Nick Prokesch
<u>Camera assistance:</u> Anna Spanlang
<u>Production assistance:</u> Denice Bourbon, Nick Prokesch

Hiding in the Lights (short film), 2013
14:00 min
4K Video, color, sound
Courtesy the artist / sixpackfilm

<u>Director, script:</u> Katrina Daschner
<u>Starring:</u> Denice Bourbon, Katrina Daschner
<u>Cinematography:</u> Hannes Böck
<u>Editing:</u> Hannes Böck, Katrina Daschner
<u>Set production:</u> Ulrich Dertschei
<u>Lighting:</u> Hannes Böck, Denise Kamschal
<u>Costumes:</u> Markus Pires-Mata
<u>Make-up:</u> Denise Kottlett, Andreas Riegler
<u>Assistant director:</u> Nick Prokesch
<u>Production assistance:</u> Denice Bourbon, Nick Prokesch
<u>Cinematography and light assistants:</u> Liesa Kovacs, Anna Spanlang
Funded by BMKÖS—Bundesministerium für Kunst, Kultur, öffentlichen Dienst und Sport

Powder Placenta, 2015
09:17 min
4K Video, color, sound
Courtesy the artist / sixpackfilm

<u>Director, script:</u> Katrina Daschner
<u>Starring:</u> Stefanie Sourial, Hyo Lee, Sushila Mesquita, Cordula Thym, Gisi Håkanson
<u>Cinematography:</u> Hannes Böck
<u>Editing:</u> Hannes Böck, Katrina Daschner
<u>Set design:</u> Diego R. Ortiz,

Jenny Schleif
Lighting: Hannes Böck
Costumes: Markus Pires-Mata
Make-up: Kali Edri,
Sunanda Mesquita,
Denise Kottlett
Production assistance:
Denice Bourbon,
Nick Prokesch
Assistant director:
Nick Prokesch
Funded by: BMUKK—Bundesministerium für Bildung, Wissenschaft und Forschung, Otto Mauer Fonds, Land Niederösterreich

Perlenmeere
[Seas of Pearls], 2016
08:37 min
4K Video, color, silent
Courtesy the artist / sixpackfilm

Director, script:
Katrina Daschner
Starring: Hyo Lee
Cinematography: Hannes Böck
Editing: Hannes Böck,
Katrina Daschner
Lighting: Hannes Böck,
Denise Kamschal
Make-up: Sunanda Mesquita
Assistant Director:
Nick Prokesch
Production assistants:
Denice Bourbon,
Nick Prokesch
Funded by BMKÖS—Bundesministerium für Kunst, Kultur, öffentlichen Dienst und Sport and Land Niederösterreich

Pferdebusen
[Horse Boobs], 2017
09:01 min
4K Video, color, sound
Courtesy the artist / sixpackfilm

Director, script:
Katrina Daschner
Starring: Gisi Håkanson,
Denise Kottlett, Hyo Lee,
Sushila Mesquita,
Noah Damian Safranek
Cinematography: Hannes Böck
Editing: Hannes Böck,
Katrina Daschner
Set design: Monika Rovan
Lighting: Denise Kamschal,
Hannes Böck
Costumes: Markus Pires-Mata,
Guilherme Pires-Mata
Make-up: Sunanda Mesquita,
Jolanda Resch
Production assistance:
Denice Bourbon
Set assistance:
Christina Lindauer
Camera assistance: Silk Graf
Funded by BMKÖS—Bundesministerium für Kunst, Kultur, öffentlichen Dienst und Sport and Land Niederösterreich

Pfauenloch
[Peacock Hole], 2018
09:36 min
4K Video, color, sound
Courtesy the artist / sixpackfilm

Director, script:
Katrina Daschner
Starring: Noah Damian Safranek, Hyo Lee,
Dorit Margreiter, Sabine Marte,
Stefanie Sourial, Veza Maria Fernández, Angela Tiefenthaler
Cinematography: Hannes Böck
Music, Sounddesign:
Sabine Marte
Editing: Hannes Böck,
Katrina Daschner
Costumes: Markus Pires-Mata,
Guilherme Pires-Mata
Make-up: Denise Kottlett,
Jolanda Resch
Funded by BMKÖS—Bundesministerium für Kunst, Kultur, öffentlichen Dienst und Sport and Land Niederösterreich

Plum Circus, 2019
12:00 min
4K Video, color, sound
Courtesy the artist / sixpackfilm

Director, script:
Katrina Daschner
Starring: Stefanie Sourial,
Noah Damian Safranek,
Katrina Daschner,
Sabine Marte,
Denice Bourbon, Hyo Lee,
Denise Kottlett
Cinematography: Hannes Böck
Sound: Sabine Marte
Editing: Hannes Böck,
Katrina Daschner
Costumes: Markus Pires-Mata,
Guilherme Pires-Mata
Set design: Monika Rovan
Make-up: Jolanda Resch,
Denise Kottlett
Assistant director:
Anna Spanlang
Funded by BMKÖS—Bundesministerium für Kunst, Kultur, öffentlichen Dienst und Sport and Land Niederösterreich

Pomp, 2020
08:00 min
4K Video, color, silent
Courtesy the artist / sixpackfilm

Director, script:
Katrina Daschner
Starring: Denice Bourbon,
Gisi Håkanson, Moira Hille,
Denise Palmieri,
Denise Kottlett, Hyo Lee,
Sabine Marte, Noah Damian Safranek
Cinematography: Hannes Böck
Editing: Katrina Daschner,
Hannes Böck
Choreography: Stefanie Sourial
Set design: Monika Rovan
Lighting: Hannes Böck
Costumes: Guilherme Pires-Mata, Markus Pires-Mata
Make-up: Jolanda Resch,
Heidi Zimmer
Production: Lady Chutney Production
Direction and production assistant: Anna Spanlang
Cinematography assistant:
Jonida Laçi
Set assistant: Alice Ursini
Funded by BMKÖS—Bundes-*ministerium für Kunst, Kultur, öffentlichen Dienst und Sport and Land Niederösterreich*

Golden Shadow, 2022
18:00 min
4K Video, color, sound,
2-channel installation,
Courtesy the artist /
Georg Kargl Fine Arts
Collection: City of Vienna

Director, script:
Katrina Daschner
Starring: Hyo Lee, Denice Bourbon, Veza Fernández, Silk Graf, Moira Hille, Laura Kind, Sabine Marte, Denise Palmieri, Noah Damian Safranek, Sarah Tseng

Works Presented

Cinematography outdoor shots: Hannes Böck
Cinematography studio shots: Caroline Bobek
Editing: Hannes Böck, Katrina Daschner
Set design: Monika Rovan
Composition: Sabine Marte
Lighting: Caroline Bobek, Germaine Haller
Costumes: Markus Pires-Mata, Maurício Ianês de Moraes
Make-up: Denise Kottlett, Jolanda Resch
Direction and production assistant: Anna Spanlang
Cinematography assistant: Jonida Laçi
Set assistant: Anna Wäger
Lighting assistant: Silk Graf
Thanks to chra (Christina Nemec) for the use of "Il Corallo"
Funded by BMKÖS—Bundesministerium für Kunst, Kultur, öffentlichen Dienst und Sport and Land Niederösterreich

Making of

Golden Shadow, 2022 (film still)

Golden Shadow, Storyboard
21 cm x 29.7 cm
Pencil on paper
Courtesy the artist

Golden Shadow, 2022 (on-set photo)

Golden Shadow
(Koralle, Palmieri)
21 cm x 14 cm
Water color and colored pencil on paper
Collection: MAK—Österreichisches Museum für angewandte Kunst

Golden Shadow
(Pearl open, Bourbon)
21 cm x 14 cm
Water color and colored pencil on paper
Collection: MAK—Österreichisches Museum für angewandte Kunst

Golden Shadow
(Feuerqualle, Veza)
21 cm x 14 cm
Water color and colored pencil on paper
Collection: MAK—Österreichisches Museum für angewandte Kunst

Golden Shadow (Krake)
21 cm x 14 cm
Water color and colored pencil on paper, Private collection

Golden Shadow (Alge, Moira)
21 cm x 14 cm
Water color and colored pencil on paper
Collection: MAK—Österreichisches Museum für angewandte Kunst

Pomp, 2020 (film still)

Pomp, Storyboard
21 cm x 29.7 cm
Colored pencil on paper
Courtesy the artist

Powder Placenta, 2015 (film still)

Powder Placenta, Storyboard
21 cm x 29.7 cm
Pencil on paper
Courtesy the artist

Pomp (Golden Shower: Take 1), 2020
30.5 cm x 18 cm
Embroidery on photo collage
Private collection

Pomp (Solidarity Legs: Scene 1), 2020
30.5 cm x 18 cm
Embroidery on photo collage
Private collection

TANZ2000 [DANCE2000], 2000
07:39 min
High-8 (8 sequences in loops), color, sound
Concept, performance, cinematography, editing: Katrina Daschner
Courtesy the artist

Collages

Take You Down to Paradise, 2000
20 cm x 15 cm
Photo collage from chromogenic prints
Courtesy the artist

Untitled (Costa), 2000
24 cm x 10 cm
Photo collage from chromogenic prints
Collection: MAK—Österreichisches Museum für angewandte Kunst

Untitled (Chiapas), 2000
10 cm x 26.5 cm
Photo collage from chromogenic prints
Courtesy the artist

Trust in Me (Fertiges Paar/Wasted Couple), 2000
10 cm x 15 cm
Photo collage from chromogenic prints
Collection: MAK—Österreichisches Museum für angewandte Kunst

Trust in Me (Sarajevo), 2000
10 cm x 15 cm
Photo collage from chromogenic prints
Courtesy the artist

Vagina Dentata, 2022
Dimensions: 2.40 m wide x 3.00 m high, variable size
Aluminum (laser cut)
Courtesy the artist / Georg Kargl Fine Arts

Photograph Credits

images on endpapers (front and back): Katrina Daschner, *Pomp*, 2020 (film stills)

p. 4/5: Katrina Daschner, *Pomp*, 2020 (film still)

p. 6/7: Katrina Daschner, *Hiding in the Lights*, 2013 (film still)

p. 18, 19, 20, 21, 22, 23, 26, 27, 66/67, 68/69, 70/71, 72/73, 74/75, 76/77, 78/79, 80/81, 82/83, 84/85, 86/87, 88/89, 90/91, 92/93, 94/95, 96/97, 98/99, 100/101, 102/103, 104/105, 106/107, 217: Installation views: "Katrina Daschner. BURN & GLOOM! GLOW & MOON! Thousand Years of Troubled Genders," Kunsthalle Wien, 2022. Photo: Iris Ranzinger

p. 24, 25, 28, 32, 33: Photo: kunst-dokumentation.com / Manuel Carreon Lopez

p. 29, 30, 31: Photo: Hannes Böck

p. 34/35: CLUB BURLESQUE BRUTAL, f. l. t. r.: Frau Professor la Rose (Katrina Daschner), Miss Bourbon (Denice Bourbon), Don Chanel (Moira Hille), Dr. Sourial (Stefanie Sourial), Madame Camel Toe (Sabine Marte), Denise Kottlett, Cunt (Noah Damian Safranek). Photo: steffi dittrich
p. 53: CLUB BURLESQUE BRUTAL: Don Chanel (Moira Hille). Photo: Ute Hölzl
p. 54: CLUB BURLESQUE BRUTAL: Frau Professor la Rose (Katrina Daschner). Photo: steffi dittrich
p. 55 top: CLUB BURLESQUE BRUTAL: Dr. Sourial (Stefanie Sourial). Photo: steffi dittrich
p. 55 middle: CLUB BURLESQUE BRUTAL, f. l. t. r.: Denise Kottlett, Cunt (Noah Damian Safranek). Photo: steffi dittrich
p. 55 bottom: CLUB BURLESQUE BRUTAL, f. l. t. r.: Miss Bourbon (Denice Bourbon), Frau Professor la Rose (Katrina Daschner). Photo: steffi dittrich
p. 56: CLUB BURLESQUE BRUTAL, f. l. t. r.: Don Chanel (Moira Hille), Miss Bourbon (Denice Bourbon). Photo: steffi dittrich
p. 57 top: CLUB BURLESQUE BRUTAL, f. l. t. r.: Cunt (Noah Damian Safranek), Denise Kottlett. Photo: steffi dittrich
p. 57 middle: CLUB BURLESQUE BRUTAL: front: Frau Professor la Rose (Katrina Daschner), back: Don Chanel (Moira Hille). Photo: steffi dittrich
p. 57 bottom: CLUB BURLESQUE BRUTAL: Frau Professor la Rose (Katrina Daschner). Photo: steffi dittrich
p. 58: CLUB BURLESQUE BRUTAL, f. l. t. r.: Frau Professor la Rose (Katrina Daschner), Don Chanel (Moira Hille). Photo: steffi dittrich
p. 59: CLUB BURLESQUE BRUTAL, f. l. t. r.: Frau Professor la Rose (Katrina Daschner), Don Chanel (Moira Hille). Photo: steffi dittrich
p. 60: CLUB BURLESQUE BRUTAL, f. l. t. r.: Miss Bourbon (Denice Bourbon), Madame Camel Toe (Sabine Marte), Denise Kottlett. Photo: steffi dittrich
p. 61 top: CLUB BURLESQUE BRUTAL: Denise Kottlett. Photo: steffi dittrich
p. 61 middle: CLUB BURLESQUE BRUTAL: Denise Kottlett. Photo: steffi dittrich
p. 61 bottom: CLUB BURLESQUE BRUTAL: front: Madame Camel Toe (Sabine Marte). Photo: steffi dittrich
p. 62: CLUB BURLESQUE BRUTAL, f. l. t. r.: Don Chanel (Moira Hille), Denise Kottlett. Photo: steffi dittrich
p. 63: CLUB BURLESQUE BRUTAL: Madame Camel Toe (Sabine Marte). Photo: Ute Hölzl
p. 64: CLUB BURLESQUE BRUTAL, f. l. t. r.: Frau Professor la Rose (Katrina Daschner), Miss Bourbon (Denice Bourbon), Denise Kottlett, Cunt (Noah Damian Safranek), Madame Camel Toe (Sabine Marte), Don Chanel (Moira Hille), Dr. Sourial (Stefanie Sourial). Photo: steffi dittrich
p. 65: CLUB BURLESQUE BRUTAL. Photo: steffi dittrich

p. 41, 45 middle: Salon Lady Chutney. Photo: private
p. 42: Salon Lady Chutney, f. l. t. r.: Stefanie Seibold, Katrina Daschner, Johanna Kirsch. Photo: private
p. 43: Salon Lady Chutney, f. l. t. r.: Carola Dertnig, Andreas Huber, Thomas Raab. Photo: private
p. 44, 45 bottom: invitations Salon Lady Chutney, 2001
P. 45 top: Salon Lady Chutney, f. l. t. r.: Rike Frank, Elke Krystufek. Photo: private

p. 47: SV DAMENKRAFT, Gustav, Sissy Boyz, 2012. Photo: Rania Moslam
p. 48: SV DAMENKRAFT, f. l. t. r.: Sabine Marte, Katrina Daschner, Gin Müller, Christina Nemec, 2006. Photo: Susi Jirkuff
p. 49: SV DAMENKRAFT, f. l. t. r.: Sabine Marte, Katrina Daschner, Gin Müller, Christina Nemec, 2006. Photo: SV DAMENKRAFT
p. 50: SV DAMENKRAFT, Gustav, Sissy Boyz, f. l. t. r.: Katrina Daschner, Sabine Marte, Gin Müller, Tomka Weiß, Eva Jantschitsch, Christina Nemec, 2012. Photo: Rania Moslam
p. 51: SV DAMENKRAFT, Gustav, Sissy Boyz, f. l. t. r.: Gin Müller, Eva Jantschitsch, Katrina Daschner, Tomka Weiß, Christina Nemec, 2007. Photo: Magdalena Blaszczuk

Katrina Daschner

is an artist and filmmaker living in Vienna. In her projects, she primarily investigates sexuality, power structures, and queer-feminist (body) politics, as well as the transfer of theatrical acts and performances into the context of exhibitions and films. She presents her projects in exhibitions, at film festivals, and in theater venues.

From 1995–2000 she studied sculpture and transmedia art at the University of Applied Arts Vienna. She also has founded and hosted performance spaces such as Salon Lady Chutney (2001–2002) with Johanna Kirsch and Stefanie Seibold; and CLUB BURLESQUE BRUTAL (2009–2014). Between 2003 and 2008, she was part of the band SV DAMENKRAFT, together with Sabine Marte, Gin Müller, and Christina Nemec.
Between 2005 and 2010, she taught at the Academy of Fine Arts Vienna.
From 2017–2019, she was a theory curator at Tanzquartier Wien (TQW), a center for contemporary choreography and performance.

Her work has won prizes like the Otto-Mauer-Preis, the Diagonale Film Prize for Innovative Film, the Outstanding Artist Award for Experimental Film, and many more.

Selected exhibitions
Kunsthalle Wien, Austria
Georg Kargl Fine Arts, Vienna, Austria
mumok kino, Vienna, Austria
Passerelle Centre d'art contemporain, Brest, France
Upstream Gallery, Amsterdam, Netherlands
Thrust Projects, New York, USA
Antonio Ferrara, Reggio Emilia, Italy
Galerie Fotohof, Salzburg, Austria
La Panadería, Mexico City, Mexico
Kunsthaus Graz, Austria
Museum of Contemporary Art, Zagreb, Croatia
Muzeum Susch, Switzerland
Wien Museum, Austria
Athens Biennale AB5to6, Greece
Zeta Gallery, Tirana, Albania
Galerie für zeitgenössische Kunst Leipzig, Germany
MUSAC—Museo de Arte Contemporáneo de Castilla y León, Spain
Museum der Moderne Salzburg, Austria
SBC Gallery of Contemporary Art, Montreal, Canada
Blackbridge Off, Beijing, China
Fundació Antoni Tàpies, Barcelona, Spain
Lentos Kunstmuseum Linz, Austria
Museet for Samtidskunst, Roskilde, Denmark
Tranzitdisplay, Prague, Czech Republic
Weserburg—Museum für Moderne Kunst, Bremen, Germany
Cobra Museum of Modern Art Amstelveen, Netherlands
RCM The Museum of Modern Art, Nanjing, China
Ex Convento del Carmen, Guadalajara, Mexico
Blurrr—International Biennial of Performing Arts, Tel Aviv, Israel
5th International Performance Festival, Minsk, Belarus
Zachęta—National Gallery of Art, Warsaw, Poland
Generali Foundation, Vienna, Austria
Candid Arts Trust, London, England
Secession, Vienna, Austria

Selected film festivals
Ann Arbor Film Festival, USA
Österreichisches Filmmuseum, Vienna, Austria
Internationale Kurzfilmtage Oberhausen, Germany
Era New Horizons International Film Festival, Wroclaw, Poland
Kasseler Dokumentarfilm- und Videofest, Germany
BIEFF—Bucharest International Experimental Film Festival, Romania
Festival MixBrasil, São Paulo, Brazil
Lesbisch Schwule Filmtage Hamburg, Germany
IndieCork Film Festival, Ireland
Clair-Obscur Filmfestival, Basel, Switzerland
Melbourne International Film Festival, Australia
Diagonale—Festival des österreichischen Films, Graz, Austria
MIX—New York Queer Experimental Film Festival, USA
Queer Lisboa, Portugal
Antimatter Underground Film Festival, Victoria, British Columbia, Canada
Kurzfilm Festival Hamburg, Germany
Busan International Short Film Festival, South Korea
identities—Queer Film Festival, Vienna, Austria
image+nation Festival Film LGBTQueer Montréal, Canada
GAZE International LGBTQIA Film Festival, Dublin, Ireland
Semana Cine Experimental de Madrid, Spain

Selected theater venues
brut Wien, Austria
Staatsschauspiel Dresden, Germany
SO36, Berlin, Germany
Tanzquartier Wien, Austria
WerkX, Vienna, Austria

Artist books by Katrina Daschner
Nouvelle Burlesque Brutal, Salzburg: FOTOHOF edition, 2012
Killing the Systems Softly, Salzburg: FOTOHOF edition, 2004
Do lesbians have better sex? Of course they do!, Salzburg: FOTOHOF edition, 2002
Jeanny, 1998 (out of print)

Documentaries, selected interviews, reviews, and publications on Katrina Daschner's works

Liesa Kovacs and Nick Prokesch, *Femme Brutal,* 2015, a documentary film about CLUB BURLESQUE BRUTAL, color, sound, 70 min.

Noll-Hammerstiel, Petra. "Katrina Daschner—BURN & GLOOM! GLOW & MOON! Thousand Years of Troubled Genders, Kunsthalle Wien." *Kunstforum International*, no. 284 (2022).

Scholl, Sabine. "Hiding in the Lights. Katrina Daschner." In *Picturing Austrian Cinema. 99 Films/100 Comments,* edited by Katharina Müller and Claus Philipp. Leipzig: Spector Books, 2022.

Kamalzadeh, Dominik. "Subversive Korallen." *Der Standard* (July 1, 2022).

Huber, Michael. "Queere Quallen besiegen die Stacheln der Sprache." *Kurier* (July 5, 2022).

Gleich, Ania. "Burn and Gloom!" *FAQ,* no. 66 (2022).

Gregori, Daniela. "Raumnovelle." *ray Filmmagazin,* no. 07 + 08 (2022).

Grissemann, Stefan. "Katrina Daschner—Kunsthaar in Unterwasserlandschaft." *Profil*, no. 26 (June 26, 2022).

Letschnig, Melanie. "Katrina Daschner—*BURN & GLOOM! GLOW & MOON! Thousand Years of Troubled Genders.*" *Springerin,* no. 3 (2022).

Braidt, Andrea B. "Weiblichkeit, Maskerade, Queerness. Zu Katrina Daschners Filmserie nach der Traumnovelle." In *Eine eigene Geschichte—Frauen Film Österreich seit 1999,* edited by Isabella Reicher. Vienna: Sonderzahl Verlag, 2020.

Gray, Carmen. "Relentless applause." *TEXTE ZUR KUNST,* no. 110 (2018).

Erharter, Christiane. "Am Ende kann große Oper stehen. Werkporträt Katrina Daschner." *kolik film,* no. 26 (2016).

Brainin-Donnenberg, Wilbirg. "Katrina Daschner—*DASCHNER.*" *Springerin,* no. 4 (2015).

Schlocker, Edith. "Opulente Kulisse für queere Rollenspielchen." *Tiroler Tageszeitung,* no. 99 (2015).

"Sculptural Bodies That Matter. Katrina Daschner's Self-Portraits. (Katrina Daschner in Conversation with Andrea B. Braidt.)" In *Self-Timer Stories,* edited by Felicitas Thun-Hohenstein. Vienna: Schlebrügge, 2015.

Meyer, Magdalena. "Keine Rollenbilder." *Die Presse/Schaufenster*, no. 43 (December 19, 2014).

Ploebst, Helmut. "Hochseilakt zwischen Genre und Gender." *Der Standard* (December 5, 2013).

"So'n Bart." *Der Spiegel,* no. 44 (2012).

Sona, Zoé. "Die Bühne als sexualisiertes Performance Feld." *Jungle World,* no. 47 (2011).

Huck, Brigitte. "Katrina Daschner—Flamingo Massacre." *artforum* (April, 2011).

Benza, Christa. "Manege frei für kultivierte Erotik." *Der Standard* (January 27, 2011).

Cerny, Karin. "Flammende Flamingos." *Profil,* no. 22 (2011).

Scheyerer, Nicole. "Wenn Hasen die Jäger fangen." *Frankfurter Allgemeine,* no. 30 (2011).

Yun, Vina. "Das ideale Publikum." *an.schläge. das feministische magazin,* no. 2 (2011).

Scheyerer, Nicole. "Wo die Busenquasteln wirbeln." *Falter,* no. 12 (2011).

Schörghofer, Gustav. "Lachen ist nicht leistungssteigernd." *Welt der Frau,* no. 1 (2011).

Hofleitner, Johanna. "Vorstellung: Katrina Daschner." *Die Presse/Schaufenster* (December 9, 2010).

Benzer, Christa. "Ganze Körperarbeit. Zu einer kleinen Auswahl jüngster Performance-Videos." *kolik.film,* Sonderheft no. 11 (2009).

Benzer, Christa. "Two lesbians with a job." (Interview with Katrina Daschner / Dorit Margreiter). In *Smell It! Freundschaft als Lebens-, Produktions- und Aktionsform.* edited by Dietmar Schwärzler. Wien: Remaprint 2009.

Spiegler, Almuth. "Dolores machts auch ohne." (Interview with Katrina Daschner). *Die Presse,* no. 18.303 (February 6/7, 2009).

Eismann, Sonja. "Penetrante Bilder." *Jungle World,* no. 16 (2009).

Benzer, Christa. "Abgefahrene Blicke." *Der Standard* (January 8, 2009).

"Katrina Daschner: 'In welchem Feld oder Bereich ich temporär mehr kämpfe, hängt bei mir von meiner jeweiligen Lebenssituation ab.'" In Doderer, Yvonne P. *Doing beyond gender. Interviews zu Positionen und Praxen in Kunst, Kultur und Medien.* Münster: Monsenstein & Vannerdat, 2008.

"Katrina Daschner. TäterIn." *31. Das Magazin des Instituts für*

Theorie der Gestaltung und Kunst, no. 12/13 (Dezember 2008).
Grzonka, Patricia. "Katrina Daschner—'Alles ist Dildo, alles ist Loch, alles ist Clitoris' (B.P.)", Bildstrecke. *Springerin,* no. 2 (2008).
Mendelsohn, Adam E. "Katrina Daschner—*Fear Eat Soul Up,* Thrust Projects." *ArtReview,* no. 19 "Special Focus: Reviews Marathon, New York. Lower East Side" (2008).
Benzer, Christa. "Provokant, nicht spektakulär. Die Installation 'TäterIn' von Katrina Daschner in der Fotogalerie Wien." *Der Standard* (January 17, 2008).
Schedlmayer, Nina. "Provokation? III – TäterIn – Katrina Daschner: Traurige Königskinder." *www.artmagazine.cc* (January 15, 2008).
Hofleitner, Johanna. "Schauplätze." *Die Presse* (December 14, 2007).
"Katrina Daschner." *The New Yorker,* Goings On: Galleries—downtown (December 10, 2007).
"'Der Dildo ist die parodistische Wahrheit der Heterosexualität'—Kunstinsert von Katrina Daschner." *dérive. Zeitschrift für Stadtforschung,* no. 21/22, (January–March 2006).
Doderer, Yvonne P. "Katrina Daschner: 'Dolores'." *Springerin,* no. 2 (2005).
Wiesauer, Caro. "Dolores." *Kurier,* Sonderbeilage (spring 2005).
Schedlmayer, Nina. "Katrina Daschner—Dolores: Liebesdrama in sechs Bildern." *www.artmagazine.cc* (June 13, 2005).
Benzer, Christa. "Pfeifen auf fixe Identitäten. 'Ver-queere' Impressionen der Kindfrau: Katrina Daschner in der Factory der Kunsthalle Krems." *Der Standard* (May 10, 2005).
Scheyerer, Nicole. "Lady Chutney's lahme Lover." *Falter,* no. 7 (2004).
"Kritiker-Umfrage." *art. Das Kunstmagazin,* no. 1 (2002).
"Aktionen, Pläne & Projekte: Salon Lady Chutney." *Kunstforum,* no. 155 (2001).
Saller, Claudia. "Performing Chutney." *an.schläge. das feministische magazin,* no. 15 (2001).
Lippitsch, Doris. "Katrina Daschner—*After she disappeared into all these playgrounds.*" *Eikon,* no. 34 (2001).
Rottenberg, Thomas. "Kunstlounge mit Zwischendeck." *Der Standard* (May 31, 2001).
Grzonka, Patricia. "Bauchtanz mit Schnauzbart." *Profil,* no. 29 (June 17, 2000).

Authors

Övül Ö. Durmuşoğlu is a curator, writer, and educator working on constructive critiques of civilization, sustainability of intersectional futures, and practices of togetherness from feminist queer perspectives. She co-leads Art in Discourse at Braunschweig University of Art with Dr. Ana Teixeira Pinto and works as a guest professor for politics and aesthetics in curating at the University of Fine Arts Münster. In 2022, Övül curated two major monographic exhibitions: "Portrait of a Movement" of Boudry/Lorenz at CA2M, Madrid (currently at Tensta Konsthall, Stockholm) and "BURN & GLOOM! GLOW & MOON! Thousand Years of Troubled Genders" of Katrina Daschner at Kunsthalle Wien. Besides editing this first catalog of Katrina Daschner's work in English, she co-edited *Stages* with Boudry/Lorenz (Spector Books, 2022). Earlier, she curated programs within the 10th, 13th, and 14th Istanbul Biennials; coordinated and organized different programs and events at Maybe Education and public programs for dOCUMENTA (13); and worked as a curator for steirischer herbst in 2018. As a writer, she contributes to magazines such as *Artforum Online, Spike,* and *Frieze*, and various exhibition publications. She currently co-curates the 4th Autostrada Biennale, *All Images Will Disappear, One Day,* in Kosovo, with Joanna Warsza.

As a curator, writer, and teacher, **Rike Frank** contributes to practices and discourses committed to curatorial histories and research, instituting, and the documentation of curatorial articulations. She is interested in temporality and textility and currently works as executive director of the Berlin Artistic Research Grant Programme and co-director of the European Kunsthalle, an institution without a space.
Publications as editor and co-editor include *Of(f) Our Times: Curatorial Anachronics* (Sternberg Press, 2019), *Ane Hjort Guttu: Writings, Conversations, Scripts* (Sternberg Press, 2018), *Textiles: Open Letter* (Sternberg Press, 2015), *Textile Theorien der Moderne. Alois Riegl in der Kunstkritik* (b_books, 2015), *Timing: On the Temporal Dimension of Exhibiting* (Sternberg Press, 2014), and *Sketches of Universal History: Compiled from Several Authors* (Book Works, 2013).

Amelia Groom is a writer who is currently in Southern California with the smell of eucalyptus trees. She is currently working on an essay about Mariah Carey's refusal to acknowledge time, a collection of essays about silence as practiced and heard from queer, feminist, and decolonial positions, and a book about Claude Cahun and Marcel Moore's art and antifascist activism read through the lenses of queer and trans ecologies. She wrote a book about Beverly Buchanan's swampy and ruinous environmental sculpture *Marsh Ruins* (1981), published by Afterall's One Work series.

Andrea Popelka (she/they) is a curator, cultural worker, and researcher. She* currently works in the curatorial department at Kunsthalle Wien and is involved in several exhibition projects there, including Denise Ferreira da Silva and Arjuna Neuman's "Ancestral Clouds Ancestral Claims." Another recent exhibition project is "Life constantly escapes" at Kunstraum Niederoesterreich. Former workplaces include the Haus der Kulturen der Welt (HKW) and ACUD MACHT NEU, both in Berlin. Popelka also teaches in the Master Critical Studies program at the Academy of Fine Arts Vienna. Popelka's research interests lie broadly in the relationship between arts and politics, with a focus on materialisms, Marxisms, race, gender, and social life.

Tim Stüttgen (1977–2013) studied film studies, fine art, and gender/queer theories in London, Hamburg, Maastricht, and Berlin. His research covered issues such as the history of pornography and post/pornography, performance art, the visual histories of Black Liberation and post/slavery, sex work, Michel Foucault, and Gilles Deleuze/Félix Guattari.
As a freelance author, he published texts in *Spex, Jungle World, Spiegel Online, Testcard, Malmoc,* and *Texte zur Kunst,* among others. As a curator, he organized the symposium *Post Porn Politics* (Volksbühne Berlin, 2006), the reader of which was published by b_books in 2009. On the relationship between sexual politics and pop culture, he organized the performance festivals Genderpop! (Athens, 2008) and Body Language—What's Queer about Queer Pop? (Hebbel-Theater Berlin, 2010). In addition to being a curator and activist, he performed as the drag queen Timi Mei Monigatti.
Further publications include *Angels of Disguise (The Abstract Aesthetics of Digital Flaneurism)* (FANTÔME Verlag, 2012, with Can Oral) and *In a Qu*A*re Time and Place: Post-Slavery Temporalities, Blaxploitation, and Sun Ra's Afrofuturism between Intersectionality and Heterogeneity* (b_books, 2014).

What, How & for Whom/WHW is a curatorial collective formed in 1999 and based in Zagreb, Berlin, and Vienna. What, how, and for whom—the three basic questions of every economic organization—concern the planning, concept, and realization of exhibitions as well as the production and distribution of artworks and the artist's position in the labor market. These questions formed the title of WHW's first project in 2000 in Zagreb—"What, How & for Whom", dedicated to the 152nd anniversary of the *Communist Manifesto*—and became the motto of WHW's work and the title of the collective.
Since 2003, WHW collective has been running the program of Gallery Nova, a city-owned gallery in Zagreb. In 2018, WHW launched an international study program for emerging artists called WHW Akademija, based in Zagreb. Since 2019, part of the collective (Ivet Ćurlin, Nataša Ilić, and Sabina Sabolović) works as artistic directors of Kunsthalle Wien in Vienna. WHW continues working in Zagreb, where activities are led by Ana Dević.

Exhibition
Kunsthalle Wien
June 30, 2022 – October 23, 2022
Curated by Övül Ö. Durmuşoğlu

Artistic Directors
What, How & for Whom / WHW
(Ivet Ćurlin • Nataša Ilić •
Sabina Sabolović)

Managing Director Stadt Wien Kunst GmbH
Wolfgang Kuzmits

Assistant to the Artistic Directors
Asija Ismailovski

Assistant to the Managing Director
Viktoria Kalcher

Sponsoring / Fundraising
Maximilian Geymüller

Curatorial
Laura Amann
Hannah Marynissen
Astrid Peterle
Andrea Popelka

Publishing
Ramona Heinlein
Nicole Suzuki

Exhibition Management
Amelie Brandstetter
Martina Piber
Flora Schausberger

Event Production
Johanna Sonderegger

Technical Management
Michael Niemetz
Danilo Pacher

Art Education
Carola Fuchs
Andrea Hubin
Michaela Schmidlechner
Michael Simku
Daliah Touré
Martin Walkner

Communications
David Avazzadeh
Katharina Baumgartner
Nicole Fölß (intern)
Adina Hasler
Wiebke Schnarr
Katharina Schniebs

Visitor Services / Shop
Daniel Cinkl
Marianne Maier
Kevin Manders
Nahid Irena Safaverdi
Elisa Stumpfer
Christina Zowack

Business Administration
Maria Haigermoser
Julia Klim
Nadine Kodym
Leonhard Rogenhofer
Natalie Waldherr

Facility Management / Infrastructure
Beni Ardolic
Osma Eltyeb Ali
Baari Jasarov
Mathias Kada
Almir Pestalic

Thank you
Katrina Daschner would like to express her gratitude to:
Ivet Ćurlin • Nataša Ilić • Sabina Sabolović
Övül Ö. Durmuşoğlu
Monika Rovan
Rike Frank
Amelia Groom
Tim Stüttgen in my mind and soul
Daniela Bily
Nicole Suzuki
Esther Räsänen
Hendrik Folkerts
Hana Ostan Ožbolt
Sabine Marte
Anna Spanlang
Hannes Böck
Catrin Seefranz
Georg Kargl Fine Arts (Inés Lombardi and Melanie Wagner)
sixpackfilm
Johanna Kirsch
SV DAMENKRAFT
Hyo Lee
Denice Bourbon
Moira Hille
Stefanie Sourial
Noah Damian Safranek
Denise Kottlett
Markus Pires-Mata
Jakob Lena Knebl
Maren Daschner de Tercero
Christel Sturm
and to my beloved family
Dorit Margreiter Choy, Sarah Tseng, and Sylvi Tseng

Head of Production Studio Daschner
Monika Rovan

Assistant Curator
Andrea Popelka

External Technicians
Harald Adrian
Scott Hayes
Dietmar Hochhauser
Bruno Hoffmann

Art Handling
Marc-Alexandre Dumoulin
Parastu Gharabaghi
Luiza Margan
Marit Wolters
Stephen Zepke

Katrina Daschner
BURN & GLOOM! GLOW & MOON!

Published by
Stadt Wien Kunst GmbH /
Kunsthalle Wien
Sternberg Press

Editor
Övül Ö. Durmuşoğlu

Managing Editor
Nicole Suzuki

Texts
Övül Ö. Durmuşoğlu
Rike Frank
Amelia Groom
Andrea Popelka
Tim Stüttgen
What, How & for Whom/WHW

Translation
Anja Büchele & Matthew Hyland

Copyediting
Megan Low

Proofreading
Anna Roos

Design
Daniela Bily / be the rhythm studio

Typefaces
ABC Monument Grotesk
Migra

Printing
Gerin Druck GmbH,
Wolkersdorf, Austria

Printed in Austria

© 2023 the artist, the authors, Stadt Wien Kunst GmbH, Sternberg Press

All rights reserved, including the right of reproduction in whole or in part in any form.

Distributed by The MIT Press, Art Data, Les presses du réel, and Idea Books

Photo credits: image on cover (front and back): Katrina Daschner, *Pomp*, 2020 (film still)

All images are courtesy of the artist unless otherwise indicated.

We thank all copyright holders for their kind permission to reproduce their material.
Every effort has been made to contact the rightful owners with regard to copyrights and permissions. We apologize for any inadvertent errors or omissions.

ISBN 978-1-915609-31-1

Published by

Stadt Wien Kunst GmbH
Kunsthalle Wien
Museumsplatz 1
A–1070 Vienna
www.kunsthallewien.at

Sternberg Press
71–75 Shelton Street
UK–London WC2H 9JQ
www.sternberg-press.com

Sternberg Press

Kunsthalle Wien is the city of Vienna's institution for international art and discourse.

kunsthalle wien